THE CARTOONING KIT!

*COMPLETE WITH CARTOON STENCILS!

PUBLISHED BY ARCTURUS PUBLISHING LIMITED

FOR INDEX BOOKS
HENSON WAY
KETTERING
NORTHANTS
NN16 8PX

THIS EDITION PUBLISHED - 1999

ISBN. 1. 900032. 59.7

CONTENTS...

WHERE DO I START ?!

DON'T PANIC—
YOU ONLY NEED TWO THINGS TO GET STARTED IN CARTOONING—

1. SOMETHING TO DRAW **WITH**...

2. SOMETHING TO DRAW **ON**...

YOU CAN DRAW CARTOONS WITH JUST ABOUT ANYTHING THAT MAKES A MARK ~ ALTHOUGH I DON'T RECOMMEND DRAWING WITH STRAWBERRY JAM!

TRY SOME OF THESE . . .

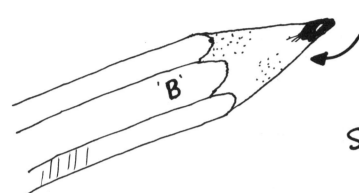

PENCIL – A FIRM FAVOURITE, AND PERFECT FOR SKETCHES AND 'ROUGHS.' USE A GRADE 'B'.

BIRO ALSO GOOD FOR SKETCHES, BUT BE CAREFUL NOT TO BLOTCH OR BLOB!

FOUNTAIN PEN

AN OLD FOUNTAIN PEN WILL WORK WELL ENOUGH FOR CARTOONING – BUT REMEMBER TO USE WATER-BASED INK OR IT MIGHT CLOG UP!!

WAIT... THERE'S **MORE**...

6

SOME CARTOONISTS USE A **BRUSH**... WHY NOT GIVE IT A TRY YOURSELF?

TECHNICAL PENS ARE QUITE EXPENSIVE - BUT GIVE A SUPER SMOOTH LINE, AND LAST FOR YEARS (IF YOU LOOK AFTER THEM!)

SOME SLIGHTLY MORE UNUSUAL DRAWING EQUIPMENT MIGHT INCLUDE...

INKY FINGERS

POINTED COCKTAIL STICK →

ARTISTS' BRUSH/PEN

BASICALLY-

IF YOU CAN GET INK ON IT, YOU CAN DRAW WITH IT!

7

YOU CAN DRAW CARTOONS ON JUST ABOUT ANY KIND OF PAPER - BUT PAPER WITH A **SMOOTH** SURFACE IS BEST...

MY NAME'S BOND

PAPER

YOU CAN BUY SKETCHBOOKS OR PACKS OF TYPING PAPER FROM YOUR LOCAL STATIONERY SHOP — OR...

BUY A **REAM** (500 SHEETS) OF **PHOTOCOPIER** PAPER FROM AN OFFICE SUPPLY SHOP.

A4 IS A COMMON PAPER SIZE IN EUROPE— **LEGAL** IS SLIGHTLY LARGER THAN A4, **LETTER** IS SLIGHTLY SMALLER.

* THERE IS MORE TECHNICAL STUFF ABOUT PENS, PAPER AND OTHER EQUIPMENT AT THE END OF THE BOOK - BUT LET'S START DRAWING NOW →

8

NW...

YOU HAVE EVERYTHING YOU NEED TO START DRAWING **CARTOONS!**

LET'S BEGIN BY DRAWING A SIMPLE CARTOON FACE, USING A FEW EASY SHAPES, LETTERS AND NUMBERS...

① START BY DRAWING ⟶ A QUESTION MARK

② NOW, ADD THE NUMBER THREE ON THE RIGHT ⟶

AND A BACKWARDS NUMBER THREE ON THE LEFT ⟶

③ NEXT, DRAW TWO LETTER 'O' SHAPES ⟶ NEXT TO THE BOTTOM OF THE QUESTION MARK

MORE···

4 NOW JOIN THE TOPS AND BOTTOMS OF THE NUMBER THREES, WITH LONG CURVES →

5 PUT A FULL-STOP IN THE MIDDLE OF EACH 'O' AND A SMALL BLOB AT THE TOP OF THE QUESTION MARK →

NOW FOR THE

SURPRISE

TURN YOUR DRAWING UPSIDE-DOWN AND CONGRATULATE YOURSELF ON DRAWING YOUR VERY FIRST CARTOON!

REMEMBER THESE SIMPLE SHAPES AS WE LEARN SOME MORE...

FUNNY FACES →

LET'S START BY DRAWING SOME **HAPPY** FACES...

IN A HAPPY FACE THE **EYES** ARE WIDE OPEN, AND THE **EYEBROWS** ARE LITTLE CURVES DRAWN ABOVE THE EYES.

THE **MOUTH** CURVES UPWARDS.

NOTICE I AM STILL USING **SIMPLE SHAPES** TO DRAW THE REST OF THE FACE.

IN A **LAUGHING** FACE THE EYES CAN BE DRAWN SQUEEZED SHUT, AND THE MOUTH MADE BIGGER TO SHOW THE **TEETH**.

ONCE YOU HAVE PRACTISED DRAWING YOUR HAPPY FACE FROM THE FRONT, YOU MIGHT WANT TO TRY DRAWING IT FROM THE SIDE - **EASY!**

START BY DRAWING YOUR HAPPY FACE IN THE USUAL WAY.

THEN DRAW A LINE DOWN THE MIDDLE OF THE FACE AND ERASE EVERYTHING ON THE LEFT HAND SIDE- EXCEPT THE NOSE AND THE EYE.

AND - HEY PRESTO- YOU HAVE A PROFILE (OR SIDE VIEW) OF YOUR **HAPPY FACE.**

PRACTISE THIS A FEW TIMES - IT'S **EASY!**

13

HERE ARE SOME **HAPPY** FACES FROM MY
OWN CARTOONS...

* WHY NOT
START UP A
SKETCH BOOK
OF YOUR OWN
FAVOURITE
FACES !?

14

NOW—LET'S TRY **ANOTHER** FACE...

WHEN WE DRAW A **SAD** FACE...

THE **EYES** ARE DRAWN HALF CLOSED.

THE **MOUTH** IS A CURVE POINTING DOWN AT THE ENDS.

THE REST OF THE FACE IS DRAWN USING THE SIMPLE SHAPES WE LEARNED BEFORE.

* SAD PEOPLE IN CARTOONS ARE SOMETIMES DRAWN WITH A GREY CLOUD OF GLOOM OVER THEM.

TO MAKE THE FACE EVEN MORE EXPRESSIVE YOU CAN **EXAGGERATE** SOME OF THE FEATURES

15

* A FEW MORE EXAMPLES

➡ TRY A FEW SAD FACES... THEN GO ON TO THE NEXT ONE....

ANGRY

FACES ARE GREAT FUN TO DRAW — PLENTY OF ROOM FOR **EXAGGERATION!**

THE **EYES** ARE DRAWN UNDER DOWN-POINTING EYEBROWS

THE **MOUTH** IS SHOWING PLENTY OF ANGRY TEETH!

IN THIS "**EXTRA ANGRY**" VERSION THE MOUTH IS A SIDEWAYS NUMBER 8 — AND I HAVE ADDED STEAM COMING FROM THE **EARS**....

＊ PRACTISE YOUR HAPPY, SAD AND ANGRY FACES —

THEN WE'LL TRY SOME MORE

16

A **SURPRISED** FACE IS VERY SIMPLE — YOU DREW ONE UPSIDE-DOWN ON PAGE 10.

THE **EYES** ARE THE SAME AS IN THE HAPPY FACE.

THE **MOUTH** IS JUST A DOT OR SMALL **OVAL** SHAPE.

IN A **PUZZLED** FACE WE HAVE.....

ONE EYEBROW UP
(LIKE THE HAPPY FACE)
AND ONE EYE HALF CLOSED
(LIKE THE SAD FACE).

THE EASIEST PUZZLED
MOUTH IS JUST A
WIGGLY LINE.

* REMEMBER
TO PRACTISE
DRAWING FACES
IN "PROFILE" AS
WELL AS FROM
THE FRONT.

17

A FEW MORE USEFUL EXPRESSIONS...

WITH ANGRY EYES AND A SMILING MOUTH WE CREATE A **SLY** FACE - **PLOTTING** SOMETHING!

TO DRAW A **BORED** FACE USE THE HALF-CLOSED EYES FROM THE SAD FACE - WITH SOME **SHADING** LINES AT THE SIDE.

FOR A **RUDE** FACE TRY THE EYES FROM THE PUZZLED FACE, PLUS A SMILING MOUTH - COMPLETE WITH TONGUE!!

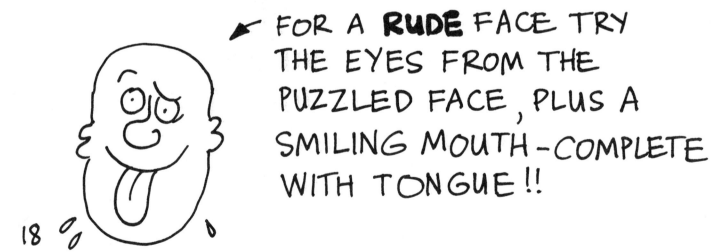

18

✱ NOW WE CAN DRAW LOTS OF EXPRESSIONS, WE CAN TURN THESE "EGGHEADS" INTO REAL PEOPLE...

HERE ARE SOME MORE FINISHED FACES YOU
MIGHT LIKE TO TRY FOR YOURSELF....

* START
FILLING YOUR
SKETCHBOOK WITH FACES AND EXPRESSIONS!

AND HERE ARE SOME BLANK FACES
FOR YOU TO PRACTISE ON:—

● TRACE OR
PHOTOCOPY
THIS PAGE...

LET'S START WITH A SIMPLE FACE . . . .

DRAWN WITH SIMPLE SHAPES — AS USUAL.

* TIME TO TRANSFORM THIS INTO OUR FIRST TWO CARTOON CHARACTERS . . .

FIRST . . .

BY ADDING A FEW FEATURES — MOUSTACHE BEARD (AND STUBBLE!) SUIT AND TIE

WE CREATE OUR FIRST CHARACTER . . . **TRY IT !**

OR . . .

BY ADDING LONGER HAIR, EARRINGS, LIPSTICK AND EYELASHES WE CREATE OUR SECOND CHARACTER →

22

* TRY THIS WITH SOME OF YOUR OWN FACES !!

✳ REMEMBER TO PRACTISE THE SIDE VIEWS OF YOUR CARTOON FACES, TOO!

YOU WILL ALMOST CERTAINLY WANT TO DRAW CARTOON CHARACTERS OF DIFFERENT AGES – SO LET'S LOOK AT HOW TO DO IT !

 OLDIES – LIKE ME –

OFTEN DRAWN WITH REDUCED HAIR – ADDITIONAL WRINKLES – ARCHED BACK – AND OFTEN WITH SPECTACLES OR WALKING STICK.

AND PERMED HAIR

SOME CARTOONISTS DRAW OLDIES WITH A SHAKY LINE. *

CHILDREN...

ARE USUALLY DRAWN SMALL, ROUND AND PLUMP, WITH THEIR FEATURES IN THE MIDDLE OF THEIR FACES...

NOT MUCH HAIR AND NOT MANY TEETH.

BIG EARS.

BIB

THEIR HEADS ARE OFTEN THE SAME SIZE AS THEIR BODIES.

* AND REMEMBER TO PRACTISE DRAWING YOUR OLDIES AND CHILDREN WITH A FULL RANGE OF THE FACIAL EXPRESSIONS WE HAVE ALREADY COVERED.

AND REMEMBER TO PRACTISE SKETCHING
EVERYONE YOU SEE AROUND YOU...

* INCLUDE EVERYONE
FROM BANK MANAGERS
TO CARTOONISTS...

TOP 5 TIPS ... FOR DRAWING FUNNY FACES ...

① PRACTISE EXPRESSIONS IN A MIRROR.

② DRAW MALE AND FEMALE FACES, OLD AND YOUNG.

③ ADD ACCESSORIES TO YOUR FACES: SPECTACLES, BEARDS, EARRINGS, ETC. ETC.

④ DRAW THE SAME FACE WITH A VARIETY OF DIFFERENT EXPRESSIONS.

⑤ DRAW A FACE GOING SLOWLY FROM ONE EXPRESSION TO ANOTHER...

FROM... HAPPY TO SAD

ANGRY TO PUZZLED ....

NOW WE HAVE LEARNED HOW TO DRAW FANTASTIC FACES IT'S TIME TO ADD THE **BODIES** WE NEED TO BRING OUR CARTOON CHARACTERS **TO LIFE**...

* BUT, OF COURSE, WE'LL GET IT RIGHT!

THE **EASIEST** WAY TO DRAW CARTOON BODIES
IS TO START WITH A SIMPLE...

MATCHSTICK SKELETON!

① **START** BY DRAWING THE **HEAD** AND **BACKBONE**.

NO! NOT THIS SORT!!

② NOW ADD THE **SHOULDERS** AND **HIPS**.

③ NEXT COME THE **LEGS**

* PUT A JOINT IN THE MIDDLE OF EACH LEG FOR **THE KNEE**.

DRAW SIMPLE SHAPES FOR **FEET**

FINALLY - ADD THE **ARMS** . . .

④

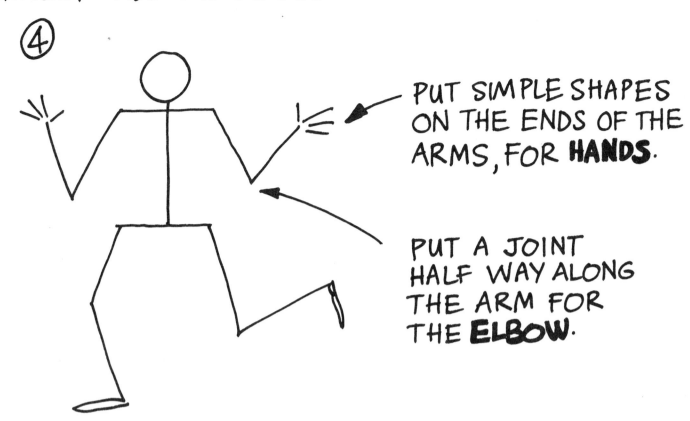

PUT SIMPLE SHAPES
ON THE ENDS OF THE
ARMS, FOR **HANDS**.

PUT A JOINT
HALF WAY ALONG
THE ARM FOR
THE **ELBOW**.

AND THAT'S ALL THERE IS TO IT, **HONEST!**

✳ WHEN YOU DRAW A STICK
FIGURE FROM THE **SIDE**
YOU LEAVE OUT THE
LINES FOR THE HIPS
AND SHOULDERS.

HANDY HINT

PRACTISE DRAWING STICK FIGURES IN ALL SORTS OF
POSES AND IT WILL MAKE YOUR CARTOONING EASIER!

IF YOU GET STUCK FOR A PARTICULAR "POSE" YOU CAN ALWAYS TRACE THE SHAPE YOU NEED FROM PHOTOGRAPHS IN NEWSPAPERS, MAGAZINES AND BOOKS

USE THIN PAPER SO YOU CAN SEE THE PICTURE THROUGH IT, THEN TRACE THE STICK SHAPES.

OR...

YOU COULD MAKE A MOVEABLE STICK FIGURE FROM STRIPS OF CARD, TWIGS OR PENCILS...

LIKE THIS ONE

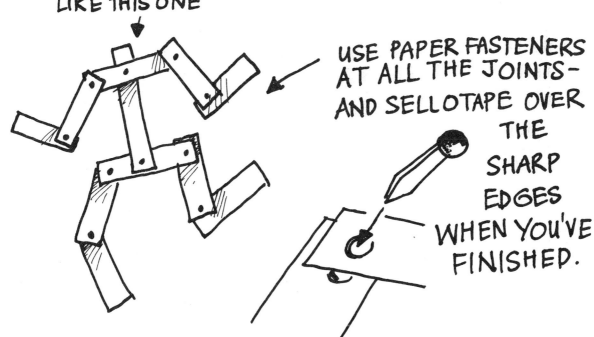

USE PAPER FASTENERS AT ALL THE JOINTS — AND SELLOTAPE OVER THE SHARP EDGES WHEN YOU'VE FINISHED.

YOU CAN HAVE A LOT OF **FUN** CHANGING THE SIZES OF THE VARIOUS PARTS OF YOUR STICK FIGURES...

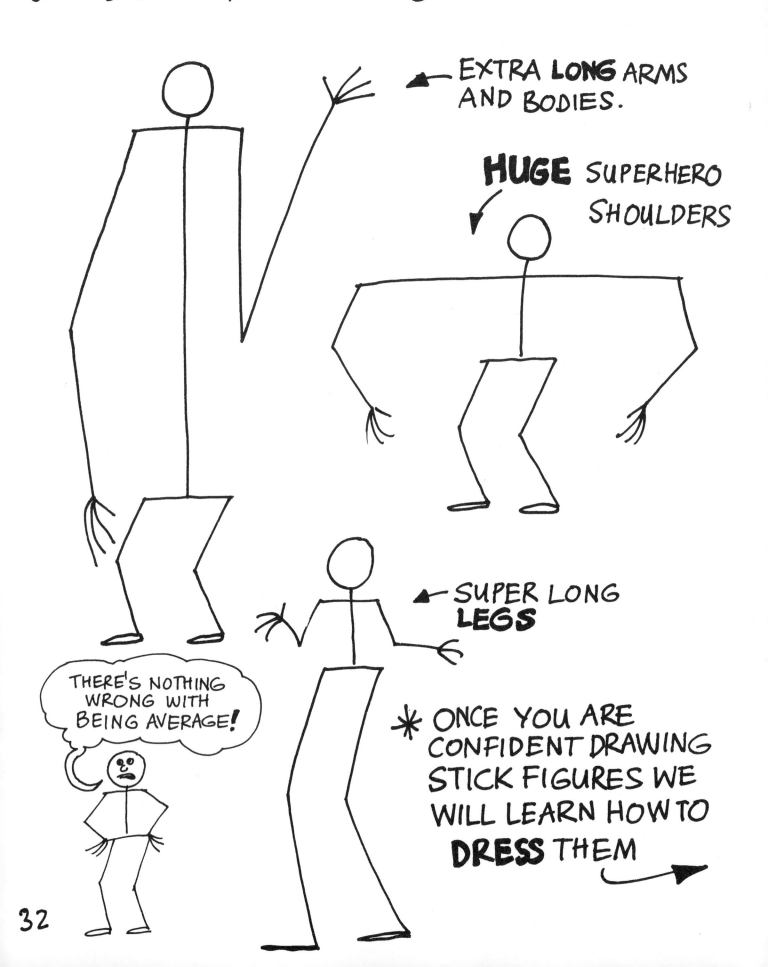

← EXTRA **LONG** ARMS AND BODIES.

HUGE SUPERHERO SHOULDERS

← SUPER LONG **LEGS**

THERE'S NOTHING WRONG WITH BEING AVERAGE!

✳ ONCE YOU ARE CONFIDENT DRAWING STICK FIGURES WE WILL LEARN HOW TO **DRESS** THEM

AN EASY WAY TO "DRESS" A STICK FIGURE IS TO
FILL THE SHAPE OUT WITH 'BLOBS' AND 'TUBES'.

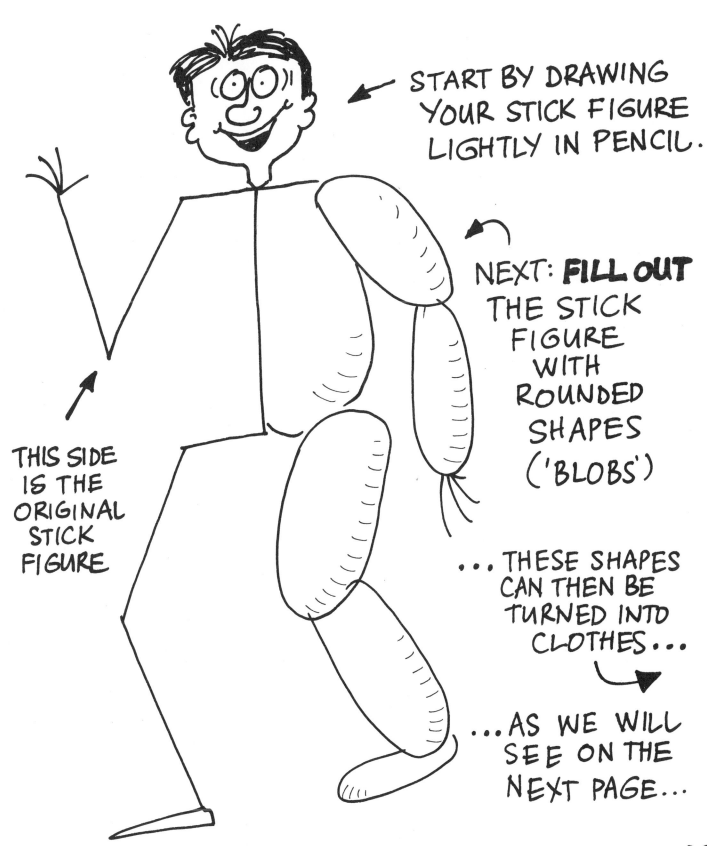

START BY DRAWING
YOUR STICK FIGURE
LIGHTLY IN PENCIL.

NEXT: **FILL OUT**
THE STICK
FIGURE
WITH
ROUNDED
SHAPES
('BLOBS')

THIS SIDE
IS THE
ORIGINAL
STICK
FIGURE

... THESE SHAPES
CAN THEN BE
TURNED INTO
CLOTHES...

...AS WE WILL
SEE ON THE
NEXT PAGE...

...KEEP THE CLOTHES NICE AND **SIMPLE** TO BEGIN WITH...

ON THIS SIDE OF THE FIGURE I HAVE STARTED ADDING SOME DETAIL TO THE CLOTHES.

ON THIS SIDE I HAVE LEFT THE 'BLOB' SHAPES.

* DON'T WORRY IT GETS MUCH EASIER WHEN YOU HAVE DONE HALF A DOZEN!

① STICK FIGURE

② ADD 'BLOBS'

③ FINISH OFF WITH CLOTHES!

HERE ARE A FEW EXAMPLES:

* START WITH THE SIMPLE STICK FIGURE - AND ADD THE 'BLOBS'!

* THE MORE YOU DO - THE EASIER IT GETS!

TRY SOME NOW!!

SOMETIMES **UNIFORMS** MAKE IT EASY TO TELL WHO IS WHO IN YOUR CARTOONS, AND YOU SHOULD PRACTISE DRAWING THEM.

DRAW THEM AS SIMPLY AS POSSIBLE - AND TRY NOT TO PUT IN TOO MUCH SMALL DETAIL ...

* YOU WILL FIND LOTS OF 'UNIFORMS' IN NEWSPAPERS AND MAGAZINES -

PERHAPS YOU COULD START A COLLECTION ?!

DAILY BLUB

KEEP A LOOKOUT FOR WHAT PEOPLE AROUND YOU ARE WEARING — **FASHIONS** COME AND GO!

* THIS IS ESPECIALLY IMPORTANT IF YOU WANT TO HAVE YOUR CARTOONS PUBLISHED!

* LOOK THROUGH MAGAZINES FOR THE LATEST TRENDS...

NOW WE HAVE LEARNED TO DRAW FUNNY FACES AND
BRILLIANT BODIES, WE CAN START TO ADD THOSE...

...ESSENTIAL EXTREMITIES!

HANDS AND FEET...

HANDS ARE GREAT FUN TO DRAW - AND IF YOU START WITH A BUNCH OF **BANANAS** THEY ARE EASY TO DRAW AS WELL!

START BY DRAWING A SIMPLE BUNCH OF BANANAS...

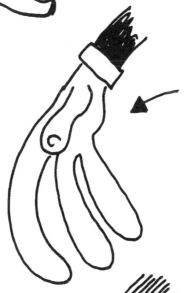

NOW - SMOOTH OUT THESE SHAPES AND ADD A "THUMB".

THE STALK BECOMES THE WRIST.

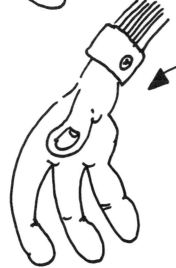

FINALLY, ADD WHATEVER DETAILS YOU WANT - BEARING IN MIND THAT YOU CAN MAKE HANDS AS SIMPLE OR AS COMPLICATED AS YOU LIKE!

I USUALLY DRAW MY CARTOON HANDS WITH 3 FINGERS AND A THUMB—BUT YOU CAN DRAW ALL 4 FINGERS IF YOU PREFER — OR EVEN MORE IF YOU WANT **!!**

* IT'S A GOOD IDEA TO LOOK AT YOUR OWN HANDS AS YOU DRAW.

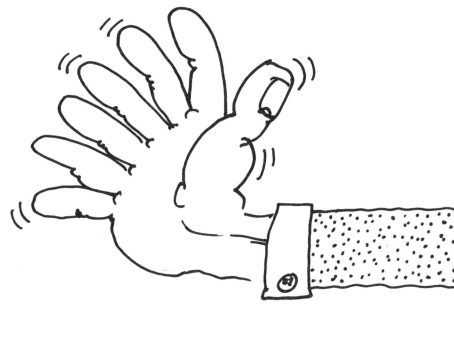

PRACTISE DRAWING HANDS IN AS MANY DIFFERENT POSES AS YOU POSSIBLY CAN.

YOU NEVER KNOW WHEN YOU MIGHT NEED THEM **!!**

EEEKK!

FEET....

CAN EITHER BE 'BAREFOOT' OR IN A HUGE VARIETY OF SHOES...

START OUT WITH REALLY SIMPLE SHAPES—

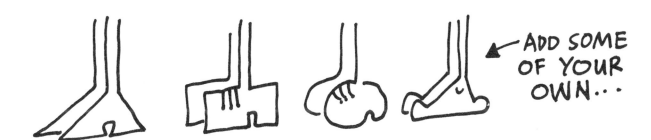

← ADD SOME OF YOUR OWN...

IT DOESN'T MATTER WHAT SORT OF SHAPE YOU SELECT—BUT IT'S A GOOD IDEA TO PUT A HEEL ON YOUR FEET — IT LOOKS BETTER.

IF YOU WANT TO ADD MORE DETAIL TO YOUR SHOES — HAVE A GOOD LOOK AT WHAT PEOPLE ARE WEARING—THEN EXPERIMENT!

TRY SOME YOURSELF...

41

WHEN YOU DRAW BARE FEET - REMEMBER - THE BIG TOE POINTS UP, THE OTHER TOES POINT DOWN...

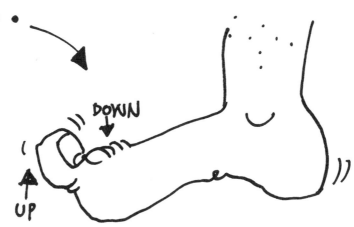

HERE ARE A FEW SHOES THAT I HAVE USED IN MY OWN CARTOONS RECENTLY, TO GET YOUR COLLECTION STARTED...

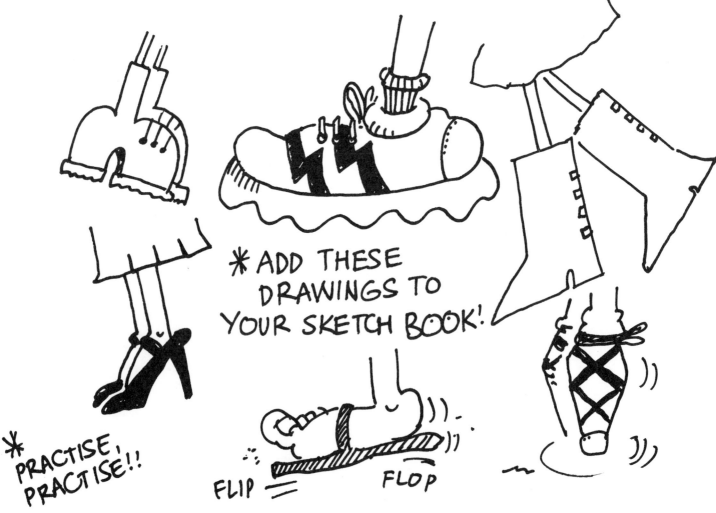

* ADD THESE DRAWINGS TO YOUR SKETCH BOOK!

* PRACTISE, PRACTISE!!

FLIP — FLOP

WOW!

NOW YOU REALLY CAN START TO PRODUCE YOUR VERY OWN CARTOONS...

WE'VE LEARNED HOW TO DRAW...

FANTASTIC **FACES** ➔

BRILLIANT **BODIES** ➔

HANDSOME **HANDS** ➔

AND

FABULOUS **FEET** ➔

*

SO NOW WE'LL LEARN HOW TO GIVE OUR CARTOON CHARACTERS THINGS TO DO...

LET'S START BY GIVING OUR CARTOON PEOPLE SOME "ACCESSORIES", OR TOYS, TO **PLAY** WITH ...

HOW ABOUT –

NEWSPAPERS, BOOKS AND MAGAZINES TO READ...
MOBILE 'PHONES AND PERSONAL CD PLAYERS TO ANNOY PEOPLE WITH...
LAPTOP COMPUTERS TO PLAY GAMES...

* I'M SURE YOU WILL BE ABLE TO THINK OF LOTS MORE THINGS...

SOME MORE THINGS TO ADD TO YOUR SKETCHBOOK!

THE PEOPLE IN YOUR CARTOONS WILL ALSO NEED TO GET INVOLVED IN PLENTY OF ACTIVITY - SO DON'T BE AFRAID TO EXAGGERATE THIS...

* REMEMBER - THE MORE THINGS YOU LEARN TO DRAW, THE MORE CARTOONS YOU CAN DRAW!

WHEN YOU NEED TO DRAW A HAND HOLDING
SOMETHING — TRY THIS METHOD ...

① SKETCH THE OBJECT BEING
   HELD, LIGHTLY IN PENCIL →

② NOW SKETCH THE HAND AROUND
   IT — AGAIN USING LIGHT
   PENCIL LINES →

③ NEXT — INK IN THOSE
   PARTS OF THE HAND THAT ARE
   IN FRONT OF THE OBJECT, THEN
   INK IN THE REST OF THE DRAWING

④ WHEN YOU ARE
   HAPPY WITH YOUR
   FINISHED DRAWING
   SET IT ASIDE TO LET THE
   INK DRY, THEN ERASE   ALL ↗
   THE PENCIL LINES.

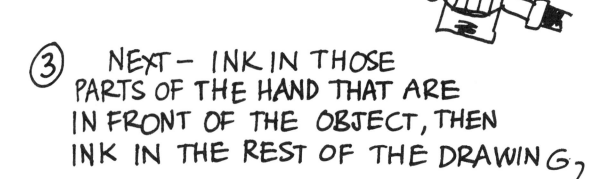

PRACTISE DRAWING HANDS HOLDING LOTS OF THINGS!

IF YOU FIND DRAWING THINGS DIFFICULT, TRY TO REDUCE THEM TO SIMPLE SHAPES FIRST ...

JUST ROUND OFF THE SHAPES!

* DON'T WORRY ABOUT GETTING THINGS "PERFECT" — THERE'S NO SUCH THING!!

* TRY SOME FOR YOURSELF... NOW!

AS WELL AS HAVING THINGS TO DO, OUR CARTOON CREATIONS ALSO NEED PLACES TO GO ...

THIS CAN BE ANYWHERE FROM A ...

... DESERT ISLAND...

← PALM TREES
COCONUTS
SHARKS
RIPPLES

TO A DOCTOR'S SURGERY ...

STETHOSCOPE
CERTIFICATES
PILLS & POTIONS

REMEMBER YOU ONLY NEED TO DRAW 3 OR 4 ITEMS TO MAKE A LOCATION RECOGNISEABLE. YOU CERTAINLY DON'T NEED TO DRAW A PAGE FULL OF DETAILS!

SO, FOR EXAMPLE, TO SHOW A SCHOOL CLASSROOM YOU COULD JUST DRAW...

A TEACHER STANDING IN FRONT OF A DESK AND A CHALKBOARD

THIS IS ENOUGH TO TELL THE PERSON LOOKING AT THE CARTOON WHERE IT IS SET!

* MAKE A LIST OF THE SORT OF THINGS YOU WOULD NEED TO IDENTIFY A VARIETY OF ROOMS AND LOCATIONS... FOR EXAMPLE...

- LOUNGE
- BANK
- PUB
- OFFICE
- RAIL STATION
- HOTEL ...

AND AS MANY OTHERS THAT YOU CAN THINK OF!

49

PRACTISE DRAWING SIMPLE BACKGROUNDS AND
LOCATIONS, AND BEFORE YOU KNOW IT YOU WILL
BE PRODUCING SUPER, PROFESSIONAL LOOKING

CARTOONS!

* HERE ARE A FEW
EXAMPLES OF
BACKGROUNDS
FROM MY OWN
CARTOONS

COMPUTER
SOFTWARE

WATKINSON
FURNITURE

PRACTISE...

TOP 5 TIPS ... FOR DRAWING

PLACES AND THINGS...

① CARRY A SMALL SKETCHBOOK WITH YOU AT ALL TIMES...AND MAKE QUICK DRAWINGS OF ANYTHING INTERESTING YOU SEE.

② DRAW THE SAME CHARACTER IN A VARIETY OF DIFFERENT PLACES.

③ PRACTISE DRAWING HANDS HOLDING AND 'USING' THINGS - YOU WILL DRAW A LOT OF THESE.

④ REMEMBER- IT IS BETTER TO 'SET THE SCENE' WITH 3 OR 4 SIMPLE THINGS.

⑤ REDUCE COMPLICATED SHAPES TO A FEW SIMPLE 'BLOCKS' TO HELP YOU GET STARTED.

CARICATURE IS GREAT FUN, AND IS EASY TO LEARN ~

* THIS IS A CARICATURE OF ME!

IT'S A GOOD IDEA TO START BY DRAWING SOME CARICATURES OF YOURSELF BEFORE LETTING YOUR PEN LOOSE ON OTHERS!

THE BEST WAY TO START IS BY FINDING SOME PHOTOGRAPHS OF YOURSELF, THEN A MIRROR, AND THEN • • • •

HAVE A GOOD LOOK AT YOUR FACE, AND NOTE WHICH ARE THE MOST RECOGNISEABLE FEATURES. YOU COULD ASK OTHER PEOPLE WHAT THEY THINK ARE YOUR MOST IMPORTANT FEATURES.

* FOR EXAMPLE...

THE SHAPE OF YOUR HEAD -

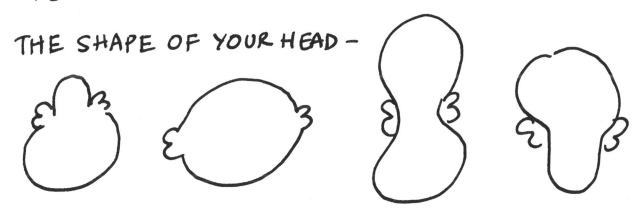

THE SHAPE OF YOUR NOSE -

THE SHAPE OF YOUR EYES -

ALSO, LOOK AT HAIR, TEETH, WRINKLES, EARRINGS ETC, ETC, ETC....

ONCE YOU HAVE DECIDED WHICH FEATURES TO USE, YOU CAN START TO "ASSEMBLE" THE FACE. (I USUALLY START WITH THE EYES AND WORK OUTWARDS)

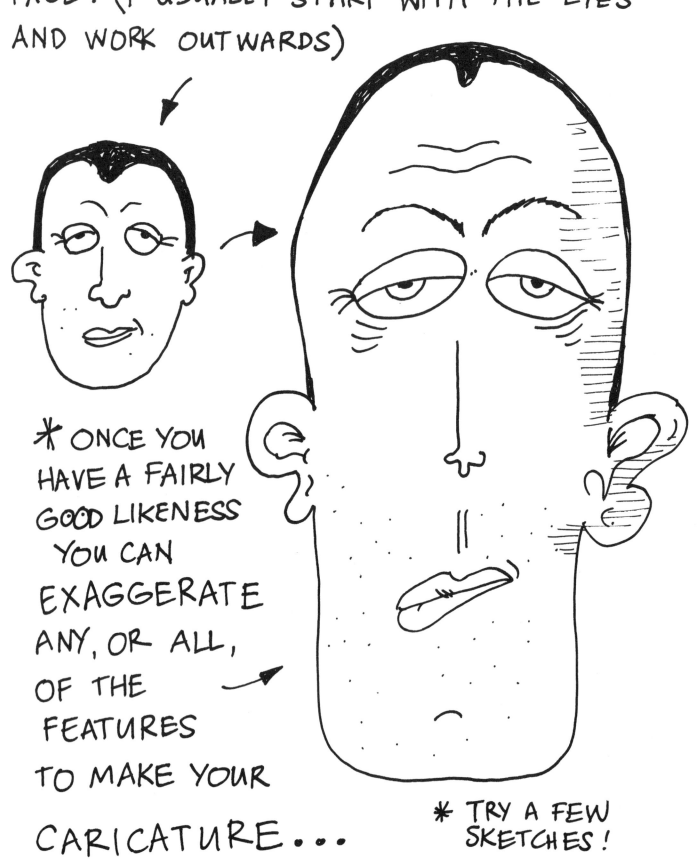

* ONCE YOU HAVE A FAIRLY GOOD LIKENESS YOU CAN EXAGGERATE ANY, OR ALL, OF THE FEATURES TO MAKE YOUR CARICATURE...

* TRY A FEW SKETCHES!

ONCE YOU HAVE DRAWN A FEW CARICATURES OF YOURSELF, YOU MIGHT LIKE TO HAVE A TRY AT DRAWING FAMILY AND FRIENDS ...

* TRY TO RESIST THE TEMPTATION TO OVER-EXAGGERATE THESE DRAWINGS - AFTER ALL, WE WANT TO ENTERTAIN OUR FRIENDS - NOT ANNOY THEM!

AND-OF COURSE- ONCE YOU'VE HONED YOUR SKILLS ON FAMILY AND FRIENDS, YOU CAN HAVE A GO AT THE **RICH** AND **FAMOUS!**

LOOK IN MAGAZINES FOR PICTURES YOU CAN USE ...

* IF YOU ARE UNCERTAIN YOUR CARICATURE WILL BE RECOGNISED YOU CAN ADD 'PROPS' TO HELP PEOPLE WORK IT OUT!

ONCE YOU HAVE THE BASICS OF A GOOD CARICATURE, WHY NOT TRY DRAWING YOUR "VICTIM" AS SOMETHING ELSE ??

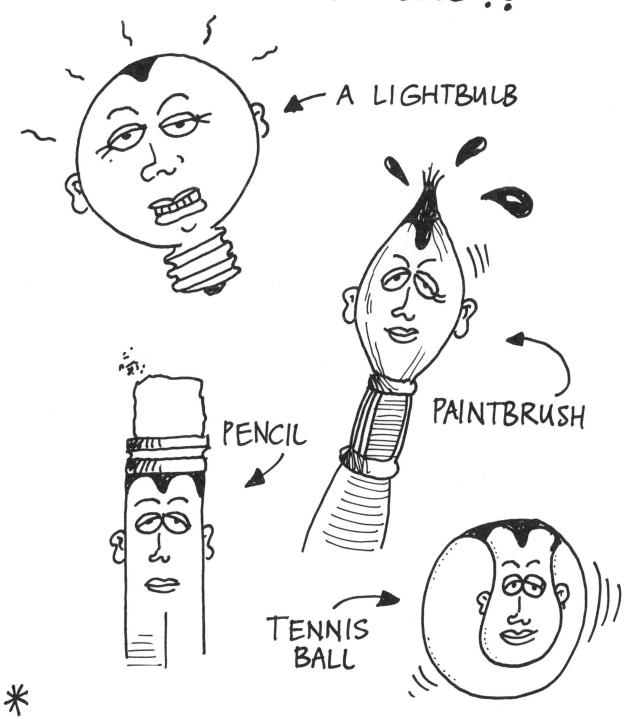

A LIGHTBULB

PAINTBRUSH

PENCIL

TENNIS BALL

* THESE CARICATURES WOULD MAKE IDEAL PRESENTS FOR FRIENDS OR FAMILY WITH PARTICULAR HOBBIES OR INTERESTS. WHY NOT FRAME ONE AS A SPECIAL GIFT!

TOP 5 TIPS ... FOR DRAWING

CARICATURES...

① REMEMBER TO LOOK AT THE DETAILS - SHAPE OF HEAD, EYES, TEETH, ETC., BEFORE STARTING TO DRAW!

② PRACTISE ON YOURSELF A FEW TIMES FIRST!

③ ADD A FEW "CLUES" TO HELP PEOPLE 'GET' WHO YOU HAVE DRAWN.

④ TRY DRAWING PEOPLE AS OTHER THINGS.

⑤ NEVER, EVER USE YOUR CARICATURES TO HURT PEOPLE - INSTEAD, TAKE PRIDE IN YOUR TALENT AND ENJOY YOURSELF!

A GOOD PLACE TO SEE CARICATURES IS YOUR LOCAL NEWSPAPER SHOP!

LOTS OF MAGAZINES AND NEWSPAPERS USE CARICATURES, AND YOU CAN QUICKLY BUILD UP A COLLECTION OF YOUR **FAVOURITE** SOAP STARS, BANDS AND FOOTBALLERS...

ANOTHER POPULAR FEATURE IN MAGAZINES AND NEWSPAPERS IS **THE STRIP CARTOON** - AND WE ARE GOING TO LEARN ALL ABOUT THEM...

...NEXT→

ONCE YOU HAVE LEARNED TO DRAW A FEW DIFFERENT CARTOON CHARACTERS YOU CAN THINK ABOUT DRAWING UP SOME FINISHED CARTOONS! **HURRAH!**

WHAT BETTER WAY TO SHOW OFF YOUR NEW CARTOONING SKILLS THAN PRODUCING YOUR VERY OWN STRIP CARTOON!

STRIP CARTOONS ARE GREAT FUN, AND YOU CAN MAKE THEM ABOUT **ANYTHING** THAT INTERESTS **YOU!**

I USUALLY START BY WRITING THE **WORDS** IN THE BOXES FIRST...

MY DOG HAS NO NOSE.	HOW DOES HE SMELL?	AWFUL!!

NEXT, I USE STICK FIGURES TO SKETCH IN THE CARTOON CHARACTERS...

61

ONCE YOU ARE **HAPPY** WITH THE LAYOUT YOU CAN DRAW IT ALL UP PROPERLY, AND THEN (WHEN THE INK IS **DRY**) ERASE THE PENCIL LINES...

THIS IS A VERY OLD JOKE — AND I AM SURE YOU WILL FIND PLENTY OF BETTER ONES.

TRY OUT LOTS OF DIFFERENT SIZED AND SHAPED 'BOXES' IN YOUR STRIP CARTOON TO MAKE IT MORE INTERESTING...

TRY PUTTING SOME OF YOUR **OWN** CARTOON FACES INTO THE BOXES ABOVE.

ON THE NEXT PAGE I HAVE DRAWN SOME MORE 'EMPTY' STRIPS FOR YOU TO **TRY OUT**...

63

YOU CAN ALSO USE PLENTY OF DIFFERENT VIEWPOINTS AND OTHER "SPECIAL EFFECTS" IN YOUR CARTOONS FOR ADDED IMPACT!

SILHOUETTES

EXTREME CLOSE-UPS

SOUND EFFECTS

SHOW THE PASSING OF TIME

SOME STRIP CARTOONS FEATURE THE SAME SET OF CHARACTERS — AND IN ORDER TO HELP KEEP THEM RECOGNISEABLE YOU SHOULD DRAW A...

CHARACTER INFORMATION SHEET LIKE THE ONE BELOW...

Brenda

BRENDA STARS IN THE HON·SEC STRIP CARTOON.

ANGRY

HAPPY

SAD

© 1998

Peter Coupe

HEAD = 1 UNIT

BODY = 1 UNIT

LEGS = 1 UNIT

HAIR

HIGH HEELS

HERE ARE A FEW STRIP CARTOON STARTS –
LET'S SEE IF YOU CAN FINISH THEM...

IF YOUR STORY IS A LITTLE BIT TOO **LONG** TO FIT INTO A STRIP CARTOON, TRY A ... ... COMIC INSTEAD !

EVERYBODY'S FAVOURITE !

REMEMBER THAT A COMIC WILL BE BETTER IF IT IS CAREFULLY PLANNED!

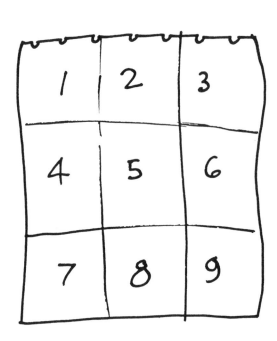

● START BY DIVIDING A SHEET OF PAPER **INTO 9** SECTIONS.

THIS IS THE 'ROUGH' SHEET, WHERE WE CAN **TRY** OUT SOME IDEAS USING JUST **WORDS**!

NEXT...

WHEN YOU ARE HAPPY WITH YOUR "STORYLINE" YOU CAN START TO PLAN OUT YOUR COMIC PAGE. INTO EACH BOX YOU SHOULD PUT THE WORDS AND ACTION THAT EACH OF YOUR CHARACTERS WILL SPEAK AND DO ● ● ●

① CHILDREN AT SCHOOL - FED UP BECAUSE THEY HAVE A MATHS TEST...

② THEY DECIDE TO PAINT THE CHALKBOARD WHITE - SO THE TEACHER WILL CANCEL IT...

③ PUPIL HOLDING PAINTBRUSH WITH WHITE PAINTED BLACKBOARD..

④

⑤

⑥

ONCE YOU HAVE COMPLETED THE 'PLOT' YOU CAN START TO SKETCH IN THE CHARACTERS USING STICK FIGURES ...

① WORDS

② SKETCH

CHILDREN AT SCHOOL - FED UP BECAUSE THEY HAVE A MATHS TEST...

I WISH WE DIDN'T HAVE A MATHS TEST TODAY!

I WISH WE DIDN'T HAVE A MATHS TEST TODAY!

TEST TODAY

③ THE FINAL RESULT - THE FIRST BOX!

I HAVE DRAWN THE FIRST 3 BOXES ON THE NEXT PAGE - HAVE A GO AT FINISHING THE STORY

WHEN YOU WANT TO SHOW THAT **TIME** IS PASSING IN A COMIC OR STRIP CARTOON, USE **BOXES** LIKE THESE...

*

I'M SURE YOU WILL BE ABLE TO THINK UP YOUR OWN BRILLIANT BOX DESIGNS!

COMIC PAGE BACKGROUNDS CAN BE SIMPLE-
SKETCHED IN WITH A FEW LINES - OR MORE
COMPLICATED AND DETAILED. IT DEPENDS ON WHAT
SORT OF COMIC YOU WANT TO CREATE...

THIS COMIC
BACKGROUND
IS VERY
SIMPLE (AND
EASY TO DRAW).

THIS
VERSION
USES MORE
SHADING
AND DETAIL

TRY BOTH,
AND PICK
THE STYLE
YOU ENJOY!

REMEMBER, TOO, THAT YOU CAN ADD YOUR FAVOURITE CARICATURES TO YOUR OWN COMIC PAGES! THIS MEANS YOU CAN HAVE ANYONE YOU WANT STARRING IN YOUR COMICS AT NO COST!!

YES — EVEN ARNIE!

WELL? WHAT ARE YOU WAITING FOR?!*@!

HERE IS A PAGE FROM ONE OF MY OWN COMICS. IT'S A SIMPLE STORY, BUT GOOD FUN! TRY ONE YOURSELF - AND BE AMAZED AT WHAT YOU CAN DO !!

WE'LL ROUND OFF THIS SECTION WITH A COLLECTION OF IDEAS YOU MIGHT LIKE TO USE IN YOUR **OWN** STRIP CARTOONS OR COMICS...

● LET YOUR CHARACTERS 'BREAK-OUT' OF THEIR BOXES TO ADD **EXTRA** EXCITEMENT

● USE EXCITING **LETTERING** TO MAKE YOUR COMICS AND STRIPS COME ALIVE!

● DON'T BE AFRAID TO USE UNUSUAL BOXES AND CRAZY ANGLES TO MAKE YOUR COMICS AND STRIPS THE **BEST**!

✱ AND NOW FOR SOMETHING **NEW** →

YOU DON'T HAVE TO DRAW JUST **PEOPLE** IN YOUR CARTOONS — THERE ARE **FANTASTIC** OPPORTUNITIES IN CARTOON LAND FOR...

ANIMAL ANTICS...

FAT CAT

AND

BATTY BIRDS...

LET'S DO IT

THE EASIEST WAY TO DRAW ANIMALS IS TO START WITH THIS SIMPLE FACE ···

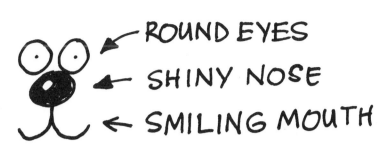

← ROUND EYES

← SHINY NOSE

← SMILING MOUTH

THIS FACE FORMS THE BASIS FOR ANY NUMBER OF ANIMALS. HERE ARE A COUPLE TO GET YOU STARTED ···

● BY ADDING A FLUFFY HEAD AND BULGING CHEEK POUCHES WE CREATE A HAMSTER

← SMALL ROUND EARS

● A PEAR-SHAPED HEAD (🧴) PLUS BIG EARS GIVES US A DOG KEEN FOR WALKIES!

MORE, MORE, MORE →

LET'S TRY SOME UNDOMESTICATED CRITTERS...

SMALL ROUND EARS AND A LARGE FLUFFY MANE...

EVEN A LION HAS THE SAME SIMPLE FACE TO START WITH

THIS CHIMP HAS A LONGER VERSION OF THE BASIC FACE, PLUS BIG EARS

WOW

• TRY A FEW OF THESE YOURSELF — START WITH THE BASIC, SIMPLE FACE AND ADD WHISKERS, TEETH, EARS, EYES: CREATE YOUR VERY OWN CARTOON ZOO!

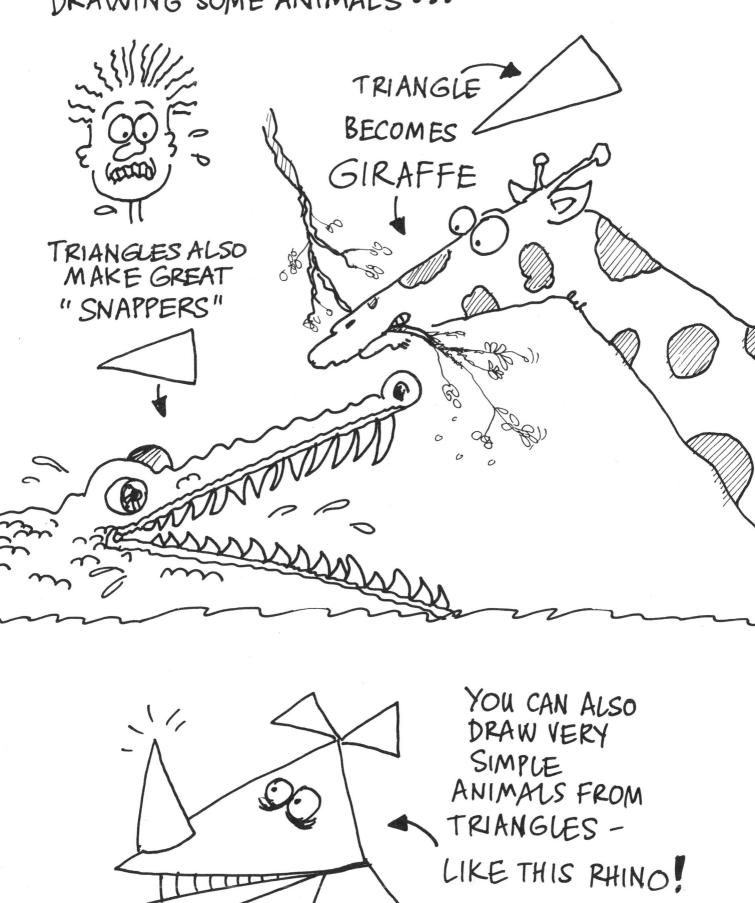

YOU CAN ALSO CREATE YOUR OWN COLLECTION OF
BATTY BIRDS FROM SIMPLE SHAPES...

A COUPLE OF SIMPLE HEART SHAPES FORM THE BASIS FOR AN OWL

SIMPLE TRIANGLES CAN MAKE BIRDS OF ALL SHAPES AND SIZES

OR TRY SOME CIRCLES AND 'BLOB' SHAPES.

REMEMBER - WHEN YOU DRAW YOUR ANIMALS AND
BIRDS - TO GIVE THEM THE SAME RANGE OF
EXPRESSIONS THAT YOU HAVE LEARNED TO
DRAW ON YOUR 'HUMAN' FACES ...

TRY
THESE
TO →
START

* YOU CAN EVEN CREATE YOUR OWN
CARTOON STRIPS AND COMICS - STARRING
BIRDS AND ANIMALS INSTEAD OF HUMANS!!

SO FAR WE HAVE BEEN DRAWING "REAL" ANIMALS ...
LET'S TRY SOME IMAGINARY ONES NOW -
TIME FOR ... **MAGNIFICENT MONSTERS!!**

LET'S START WITH SOME HORRIBLY FAMILIAR FACES...

FRANKENSTEIN'S
MONSTER IS MADE
UP FROM SPARE
PARTS - SO YOU
CAN DRAW THE
FEATURES ALL
DIFFERENT
SIZES ➤

● REMEMBER TO PUT THE BOLT THROUGH
HIS NECK - BECAUSE HE WOULD LOSE HIS
HEAD IF IT WASN'T BOLTED ON **!**

◄ START WITH A SIMPLE
RECTANGLE FOR THIS
FACE.

● REMEMBER TO
GIVE HIM LOTS
OF **SCARS** - AND
CROOKED TEETH!

A AAAARRGGHHH H H

MS. FRANKENSTEIN IS ALSO WEARING A BOLT AND VERY POOR QUALITY SPARE-PART SURGERY — BUT HAS A GREAT HAIR STYLE!

* START THIS FACE WITH A TRIANGLE AND A CIRCLE LIKE THIS ⟶

THE BOLT IS JUST A...

WIGGLY RECTANGLE WITH LINES ACROSS IT.

NOW
*
DRAW SOME MONSTER FACES AND ADD THEM TO YOUR COLLECTION

... HUR HUR HUR ....

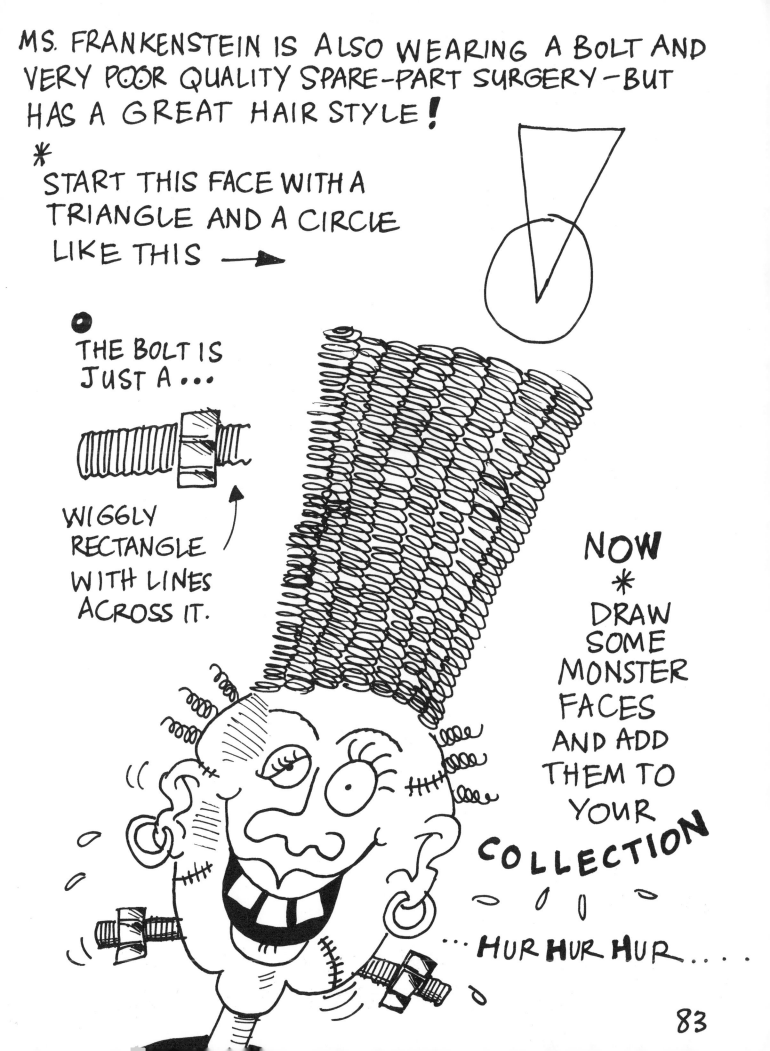

WOLFMAN

IS ALSO GREAT FUN TO CARTOON, AND WILL GIVE YOU TONS OF PRACTICE DRAWING **FUR!**

* START WITH THE SIMPLE ANIMAL FACE WE LEARNED EARLIER

THEN

ADD SOME "HUMAN" EARS AND FILL THE REST OF THE FACE AND BODY WITH FUR **!!**

DRAW A LONG NOSE WHEN YOU DRAW HIM IN PROFILE.

84

THEN, OF COURSE, THERE ARE ALL THE WONDERFUL **ANIMAL MONSTERS** ...

* THESE CAN INCLUDE
SEA MONSTERS
DINOSAURS
AND THE ODD
SHAPELESS BLOB
WITH LOTS OF
SHARP TEETH!

YOU CAN
TURN ANYTHING
INTO A MONSTER...

EVEN
YOURSELF!

86

AND WE MUSTN'T FORGET ALL THE WONDERFUL MONSTER OPPORTUNITIES THAT EXIST IN SCIENCE-FICTION AND OUTER SPACE .... BEAM ME UP!

● ALIENS CAN BE EVERYTHING

FROM

SIMPLE TIN-MEN

..TO ODD, MULTI-HANDED **ALIENS!**

87

GHOSTS ARE SIMPLE **FLOATY** SHAPES - AND YOU CAN SOMETIMES **SEE** THROUGH THEM...

* **WITCHES** ARE ALSO GREAT FUN TO DRAW, WITH POINTY **HATS**, BAD **TEETH** AND A VARIETY OF SKIN DISORDERS,

OH! AND NOT FORGETTING SKELETONS

88

YOU CAN ALSO BRING OTHER THINGS
TO LIFE — PENS AND PENCILS,
COMPUTERS, TEAPOTS, GOLF CLUBS,
EVEN TALKING
SHOES!

START WITH A SIMPLE
SKETCH OF THE
OBJECT YOU WANT TO
BRING TO LIFE — THEN
ADD EXPRESSIONS
AND GESTURES TO
SUIT THE CHARACTER.

REMEMBER TO
USE SIMPLE SHAPES
▭ △ ◯ ⬭
TO HELP YOU
BUILD
THE
CARTOON.

TOP 5 TIPS ... FOR DRAWING

ANIMALS, BIRDS AND MONSTERS!

① USE SIMPLE SHAPES TO HELP GET STARTED— SQUARES, TRIANGLES, HEARTS, CIRCLES...

② DON'T BE AFRAID TO LET YOUR IMAGINATION RUN RIOT — ESPECIALLY WITH MONSTERS!!

③ PRACTISE DRAWING DETAILS LIKE HAIR, FUR, TEETH (AND FANGS), SCALES, ETC.

④ CARRY YOUR SKETCHBOOK — AND USE IT!

⑤ MIX TOGETHER DIFFERENT PARTS OF DIFFERENT ANIMALS AND SEE WHAT YOU GET!

THERE WILL COME A TIME WHEN YOU NEED TO PUT SOME WORDS ON YOUR CARTOONS. **EASY!** IF YOU LOOK BACK THROUGH THIS BOOK YOU WILL SEE A VARIETY OF WAYS OF DOING THIS.

Some Cartoonists use Upper and Lower Case Letters in Their Cartoons...

OTHERS,- LIKE ME, ONLY USE CAPITALS.

THE IMPORTANT THING IS TO MAKE IT EASY TO READ!

NOT LIKE THIS

WHEN USING A BUBBLE - WRITE THE WORDS **FIRST!**

TO ENSURE THAT YOUR WORDS WILL **FIT!**

THEN DRAW THE BUBBLES ROUND THEM.

IF YOUR **HAND** WRITTEN TEXT IS STILL NOT AS **GOOD** AS YOU WOULD LIKE IT TO BE YOU COULD USE A **STENCIL** (FROM A STATIONERY SHOP) OR — IF YOU ARE LUCKY ENOUGH TO HAVE ACCESS TO A **COMPUTER** AND **PRINTER** — PRINT THE WORDS OUT AND **GLUE** THEM ONTO YOUR CARTOON.

...and this is what it might look like when it's printed !

REMEMBER TO USE DIFFERENT DESIGNS OF SPEECH BUBBLE TO HELP CONVEY YOUR MEANING ...

HHMMM?

SOFT, FLUFFY SPEECH BUBBLE USUALLY MEAN 'SOMEONE IS THINKING'

GET OUT!

EXPLODING AND SHARP EDGED BUBBLES ARE USED FOR SHOUTING, LOUD NOISES AND NAUGHTY WORDS!!

*?#@!

HUR HUR...

STICKY, DRIPPING BUBBLES WILL LOOK GOOD IN MONSTER CARTOONS.

- OR DESIGN YOUR OWN SPECIAL BUBBLES!

*

AS WELL AS THE WORDS IN SPEECH BUBBLES YOU CAN ALSO HAVE FUN WITH OTHER WORDS ➤

ZAP

YOU CAN USE LOTS OF DIFFERENT STYLES OF LETTERING - TO SHOW DIFFERENT **ACTIONS!**

SOFT

NNN

TRY OUT LOTS OF THESE **IDEAS** - YOU NEVER KNOW . . .

OOYYEEENS . . . **WHEN** THEY MIGHT COME IN HANDY !

WOW

ZOOM

* **START** YOUR OWN COLLECTON OF **ACTION** LETTERING . . . .

TOP 5 TIPS ... FOR DRAWING

STRIP CARTOONS AND COMICS

① USE LOTS OF DIFFERENT BOXES AND SPECIAL EFFECTS IN YOUR COMICS AND STRIPS.

② WRITE WORDS NEATLY AND CLEARLY, OR PRINT THEM OUT AND PASTE THEM IN.

③ INCLUDE CARICATURES, MONSTERS, ALIENS AND ANYTHING ELSE YOU LIKE!

④ GIVE YOUR COMIC OR STRIP CARTOON A GOOD TITLE TO GET IT OFF TO A GREAT START.

⑤ USE STICK FIGURES TO LAY OUT BOXES BEFORE FINAL INKING IN.

SO FAR WE HAVE ONLY DRAWN STATIC
CARTOONS - **NOW** WE ARE GOING TO LEARN
HOW TO MAKE OUR CHARACTERS COME TO
LIFE WITH SOME...

AWESOME

ANIMATION

LET'S MAKE MOVING PICTURES...

PENCIL FLIPS ARE GREAT **FUN** AND SIMPLE TO MAKE...

START BY CUTTING A PIECE OF THICK PAPER OR THIN CARD TO 250mm by 50mm

250 × 50

NEXT, FOLD THIS IN THE MIDDLE, THEN DRAW TWO CARTOONS, ONE ON EACH OF THE **FLAPS** MARKED WITH A ✳

FOLDED

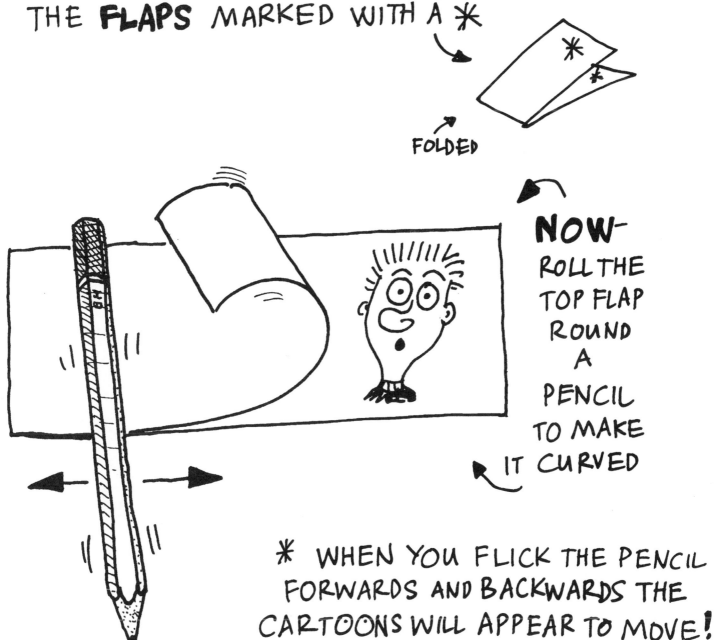

NOW ROLL THE TOP FLAP ROUND A PENCIL TO MAKE IT CURVED

✳ WHEN YOU FLICK THE PENCIL FORWARDS AND BACKWARDS THE CARTOONS WILL APPEAR TO MOVE!

A SLIGHTLY MORE SOPHISTICATED FORM OF THE PENCIL FLIP IS THE

FLICKER BOOK...

① DRAW A SIMPLE **FACE** ON THE LAST PAGE OF A SKETCHBOOK.

② GO **BACK** A PAGE AND DRAW THIS SAME FACE AGAIN - BUT WITH ONE OR TWO VERY SLIGHT CHANGES.

③ WHEN YOU HAVE DRAWN 20 OR 30 PAGES, **FLICK** THE BOOK AND WATCH YOUR CARTOONS COME TO LIFE!

● START WITH SOMETHING **SIMPLE** -
SOMEONE OPENING
AND CLOSING
THEIR EYES
OR MOUTH...

SEE THE EXAMPLE

DO ONE **NOW**!

PENCIL SPINNERS ARE ANOTHER **EASY** TO MAKE ANIMATION DEVICE...

● JUST CUT OUT TWO CIRCLES OF THIN **CARD**, AND DRAW TWO DIFFERENT PICTURES ON EACH ONE...

NEXT-

TAPE THE DRAWINGS EITHER SIDE OF A PEN OR PENCIL, AND **TWIST** BETWEEN YOUR FINGERS, OR ROLL ALONG THE EDGE OF A DESK OR TABLE, TO SEE **ACTION!**

● START WITH SIMPLE IDEAS - LIKE A FIREWORK EXPLODING OR AN EGG BREAKING OPEN

TO MAKE THE SORT OF ANIMATED CARTOON YOU SEE ON T.V. OR AT THE CINEMA, A SERIES OF IMAGES - EACH ONE SLIGHTLY DIFFERENT - ARE PROJECTED QUICKLY ON TO A SCREEN. AS THE BRAIN CAN'T KEEP UP WITH THE EVER CHANGING IMAGES IT SIMPLY LETS THEM FLOW TOGETHER - GIVING THE IMPRESSION OF MOVEMENT!

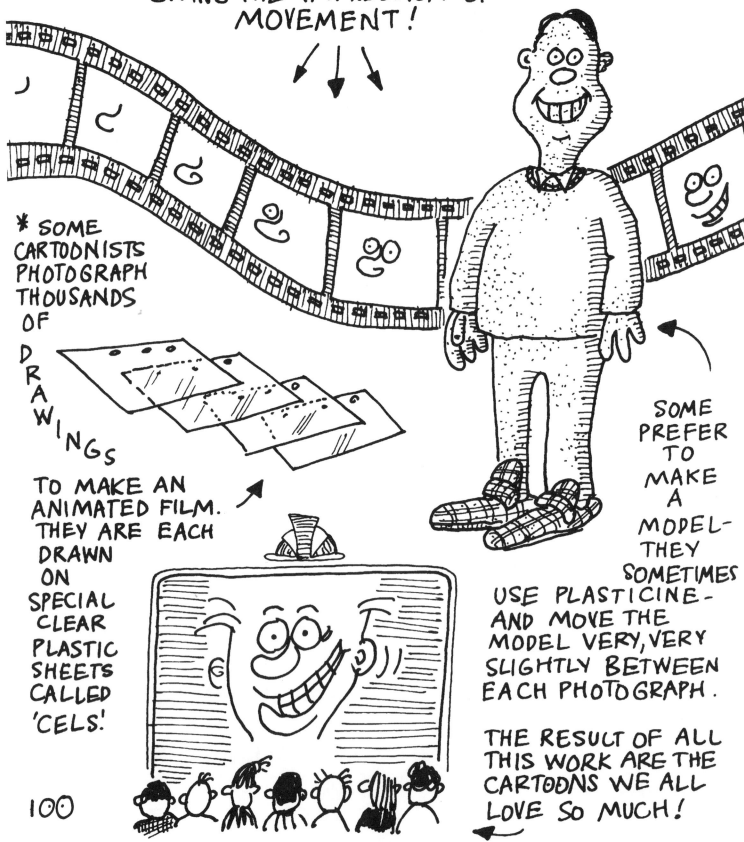

* SOME CARTOONISTS PHOTOGRAPH THOUSANDS OF DRAWINGS TO MAKE AN ANIMATED FILM. THEY ARE EACH DRAWN ON SPECIAL CLEAR PLASTIC SHEETS CALLED 'CELS!'

SOME PREFER TO MAKE A MODEL - THEY SOMETIMES USE PLASTICINE - AND MOVE THE MODEL VERY, VERY SLIGHTLY BETWEEN EACH PHOTOGRAPH.

THE RESULT OF ALL THIS WORK ARE THE CARTOONS WE ALL LOVE SO MUCH!

100

NOW IT'S TIME TO MOVE UP A GEAR, AND LEARN SOME DRAWING SKILLS THAT WILL MAKE YOUR CARTOONS LOOK EVEN MORE PROFESSIONAL...

TIME FOR SOME...

TRULY TERRIFIC TECHNIQUES!

- SHADING
- SOLID BLACK
- VIEWPOINT
- FOCUS AND
- IDEAS ...

... AMONG **OTHERS** !

PENCIL AT THE READY...

SHADING ADDS DEPTH, AND MAKES YOUR CARTOONS LOOK MORE **SOLID**...

● SOME **BASIC** SHADING PATTERNS...

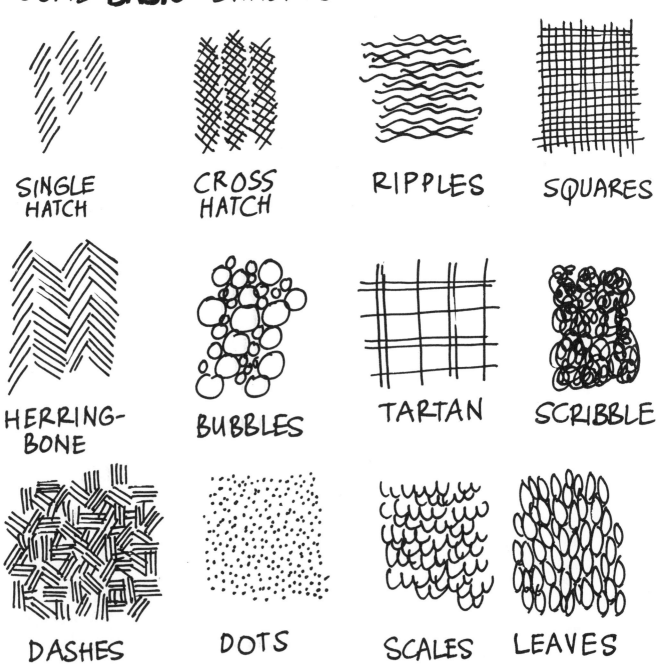

SINGLE HATCH   CROSS HATCH   RIPPLES   SQUARES

HERRING-BONE   BUBBLES   TARTAN   SCRIBBLE

DASHES   DOTS   SCALES   LEAVES

✱ THIS IS A GOOD SELECTION TO LEARN TO BEGIN WITH - ADD YOUR **OWN** LATER ...

TRY NOT TO GET TOO CARRIED AWAY WITH TEXTURES, OR YOU COULD OBSCURE YOUR WONDERFUL DRAWINGS!

JUST USE IT SPARINGLY...

● LIKE THIS →
THIS CARTOON HAS A SMALL AMOUNT OF SHADING IN IT...

* KEEP THAT PEN UNDER CONTROL!

NOT LIKE THIS →

● THERE IS TOO MUCH SHADING IN THIS CARTOON-MAKING IT DIFFICULT TO SEE WHAT THE DRAWING IS ABOUT!?!

SOLID BLACK IS ALSO USEFUL...
USE IT TO FILL IN DARK AREAS OR DARK CLOTHING...

BLACK BERET

DARK OUTSIDE

YOU CAN ALSO USE BLACK TO 'HIGHLIGHT' LIGHTER AREAS

BLACK TROUSERS AND 'T' SHIRT

BLACK BACKGROUND SHOWS UP THE BLONDE HAIR.

I LIKE BLACK!

104

BY USING A VARIETY OF DIFFERENT

VIEWPOINTS

YOU CAN MAKE YOUR CARTOONS REALLY EYE-CATCHING AND SPECTACULAR...

● LET'S START WITH A **BIRD'S** EYE VIEW →

...LIGHTLY DRAW A 'V' SHAPE IN PENCIL THEN DRAW YOUR CARTOON **INSIDE** IT

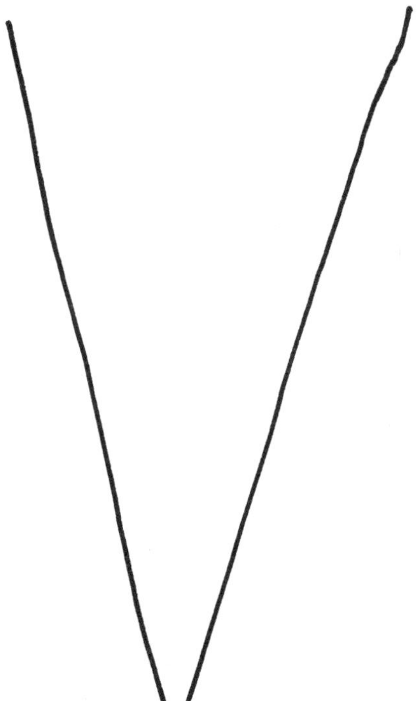

* HERE'S ONE I DREW EARLIER →

GREAT FUN!

IF YOU TURN THE 'V' SHAPE UPSIDE DOWN YOU CAN DRAW A 'WORM'S EYE VIEW'...

TRY IT –
IT'S GREAT–
AND IT'S
EASY!

AGAIN, START
WITH THE SHAPE
DRAWN IN
LIGHT **PENCIL**–

WHICH WILL
RUB OUT
EASILY WHEN
YOUR DRAWING
IS COMPLETE.

YOU CAN USE THIS CLEVER EFFECT **ACROSS** THE PAGE AS WELL, TO GIVE YOU SIMPLE...

PERSPECTIVE...

● START WITH A TRIANGLE POINTING TO THE RIGHT, LIKE THIS

✱ DRAW THIS IN PENCIL AND RUB IT OUT WHEN THE CARTOON IS FINISHED

● USE THIS TECHNIQUE WHERE YOU NEED TO DRAW STREET SCENES, OR HAVE PEOPLE FOLLOWING EACH OTHER

✱ IT CAN ALSO BE USED TO MAKE DRAMATIC CARTOONS →

HERE ARE A COUPLE OF EXAMPLES...

THE HUMAN CANNONBALL

TUNNEL VISION

TRY A FEW OF THESE BEFORE YOU LEAVE!

FOCUS IS A WAY OF DIRECTING PEOPLE TO THE IMPORTANT PART OF YOUR **CARTOON**.

● THE EASIEST WAY TO DO THIS IS TO DRAW THE MAIN SUBJECT IN A **THICKER** LINE THAN THE REST OF THE CARTOON...

LIKE THESE →

DISTORTION IS GREAT **FUN** - AND SOOOO **EASY** TO DO ● ● ●

● START WITH A 'NORMAL' CARTOON...

THEN... DRAW A GRID OVER THE CARTOON -

ABOUT 16 TO 20 SQUARES IS ABOUT RIGHT.

NOW (THE CLEVER BIT) DRAW THE GRID OUT AGAIN - BUT TWIST AND BEND IT OUT OF SHAPE

HERE'S AN EXAMPLE ....

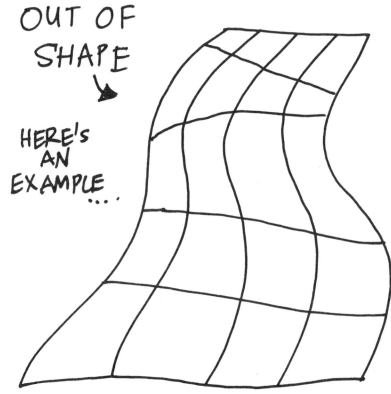

NOW - COPY THE FACE INTO THE NEW GRID - ONE SQUARE AT A TIME - AND SEE WHAT YOU GET

WHEN THE INK IS DRY, RUB OUT THE PENCIL LINES AND BE AMAZED AT YOUR CREATION!

● YOU CAN USE THE SAME TECHNIQUE ON OBJECTS AS WELL AS PEOPLE — TO MAKE THEM LOOK AS THOUGH THEY ARE TRAVELLING THROUGH A **TIME - WARP!**

TRY IT NOW. IT'S EASY AND **FUN!**

IT'S A GOOD IDEA TO LEARN HOW TO THINK UP YOUR **OWN** **IDEAS** FOR CARTOONS...

OVER THE NEXT FEW PAGES I WILL SHOW YOU SOME OF THE WAYS THAT I **THINK** UP IDEAS FOR MY CARTOONS...

... THAT SHOULD **FILL THE GAP**!

CONTRASTS ARE A GOOD PLACE TO START...

●

THINK ABOUT ... LARGE AND SMALL
FAST AND SLOW
TALL AND SHORT
HOT AND COLD

FOR EXAMPLE.

* **MIX** TOGETHER COMBINATIONS OF THINGS THAT **DON'T** NORMALLY GO TOGETHER...
...A BOXER AND A BALLET DANCER **?**

CHUG CHUG

VISUAL CARTOONS RELY ON JUST PICTURES TO MAKE PEOPLE LAUGH...

(ALTHOUGH YOU ARE ALLOWED TO CHEAT A BIT AND INCLUDE SOME SIGNS AS CLUES SOMETIMES!)

PHEW!!

KEEP OFF THE GRASS

BLOGGS BRUSHES STAFF GAMES ROOM

DO-IT-YOURSELF JOKE GENERATOR ...

		Food Mixer	Laughing
Police Officer	The Moon	Exhaust Pipe	Crying
Bricklayer	Pub	Television	Cutting
Teacher	Restaurant	Remote control	Carrying
Politician	Classroom	Washing Machine	Building
Traffic Warden	Graveyard	Computer	Eating
Postie	Camp site	Spade	Being Ill
Cyclist	TV Studio	Gun	Laughing
Motorist	Wedding	Circus High Wire	Running
Butcher	Shop	Catapult	Kicking
Baker	Motorway	Fishing Rod	Buying/Selling
Fishmonger	Garage	Kite	Lifting
Grocer	Swimming Pool	Guitar	Hitting
Farmer	Field	Kitchen Sink	Thinking
Mountaineer	Cinema	Tent	Looking
Potholer	Kitchen	Microphone	Waving
Computer User	Bathroom	Saw	Jumping
Cartoonist	On a Roof	Wetsuit	Sleeping
Disc Jockey	Under a Car		

PHOTOCOPY THIS PAGE...

HOW TO USE YOUR **JOKE** GENERATOR...

1... PHOTOCOPY THE JOKE GENERATOR PAGE.

2... CUT ROUND THE DOTTED LINES TO RELEASE EACH JOKE INGREDIENTS

3... MAKE FOUR PILES OF INGREDIENTS:

    i PEOPLE
    ii PLACES   ◄ PUT THESE FACE DOWN ON A DESK OR TABLE.
    iii THINGS
    iv ACTIONS

4... PICK UP ONE INGREDIENT FROM EACH PILE, AND SEE IF ANY OF THE CRAZY COMBINATIONS SPARK OFF A JOKE IDEA...

Police Officer	Kite	Gun	Waving
Motorist	Kitchen Sink	Camp site	Kicking
Cartoonist	Food Mixer	Classroom	Sleeping

5... USE THE JOKE GENERATOR AT REGULAR INTERVALS TO KEEP THE IDEAS FLOWING!

FOR EXAMPLE — USING . . .

CARTOONIST/FOOD MIXER/CLASSROOM/SLEEPING
YOU MIGHT COME UP WITH A JOKE LIKE THIS . . .

AH! I SEE HE'S PREPARING SOME IDEAS FOR THIS AFTERNOON'S CLASS!

YOU CAN ADD YOUR OWN INGREDIENTS TO THE JOKE GENERATOR — AND IF YOU ARE REALLY CLEVER YOU COULD FIND A WAY TO PUT IT ON A COMPUTER, AND WAKE UP TO A FRESH SET OF JOKE IDEAS EVERY DAY!

— TRY THE JOKE GENERATOR, NOW . . .

IF YOU FIND YOURSELF COMPLETELY UNABLE TO THINK UP **ANY** CARTOON IDEAS, TRY SOME...

CLICHES

- THESE ARE CARTOON SITUATIONS THAT ARE USED OVER AND OVER AGAIN, BUT ARE STILL **FUNNY**!

FOR EXAMPLE
- DESERT ISLANDS
- WAITING ROOMS
- CLASSROOMS
- ABOMINABLE SNOWMEN
- ALIENS LANDING ETC. ETC. ETC.

AS WELL AS THE TERRIFIC TECHNIQUES
WE HAVE JUST COVERED, YOU CAN ALSO
IMPROVE YOUR CARTOONS BY USING SOME...

TRICKS OF THE TRADE!

THESE ARE CLEVER WAYS OF SAVING WORDS, AND
USING PICTURES INSTEAD.

● FOR EXAMPLE - TO SHOW SOMEONE
SHAKING WITH ANGER WE USE
"SHAKE LINES" ... LIKE THIS...

SHAKE RATTLE AND ROLL......

TWO OR THREE
LITTLE LINES
LIKE THIS,
MAKE THE
FACE SHAKE.
HERE IT IS WITH
ANGER - BUT
IT COULD ALSO BE
WITH FEAR OR NERVES
OR COLD OR HAPPINESS

HERE ARE SOME MORE 'SHAKING' FACES -
TRY SOME YOURSELF

HAPPINESS...

FEAR OR NERVES...

GULP

FREEZING...

CHATTER
CHATTER

● NOTE THAT IN THE
CARTOON OF **FEAR**
I HAVE ALSO ADDED
BEADS OF SWEAT, AND
A "GULP", AND IN THE
FREEZING CARTOON
I HAVE ADDED SOME
ICICLES. LITTLE
EXTRAS LIKE THIS HELP
TO CONVEY THE MEANING!

THERE ARE SOME GREAT WAYS TO SHOW MOVEMENT IN A CARTOON. "ZOOM" LINES AND "CLOUDS" ARE MY FAVOURITES...

IN THIS CARTOON I HAVE USED "ZOOM" LINES -

LITTLE SETS OF 2 OR 3 LINES THAT STREAK OUT BEHIND HIM TO SHOW HIS MOVEMENT.

LEANING FORWARD = MORE SPEED

BY ADDING SMALL CLOUDS WE CAN MAKE THIS JOGGER RUN FASTER!!

AMAZING!

WHEN PEOPLE HAVE **IDEAS** IN A CARTOON, WE STILL USE A **LIGHTBULB** TO SHOW IT—

...LIKE THIS ↘

THERE ARE **OTHER** THINGS THAT WE USE ABOVE CARTOON CHARACTERS' HEADS

LIKE...
CLOUDS OF GLOOM...

BUT THEN – THE SUN CAN SOMETIMES BREAK THROUGH AND MAKE OUR CARTOON WORLD AN EVEN **BETTER** PLACE!

HERE ARE A FEW MORE TO TRY —

WAVY LINES CAN MEAN A **STRONG PONG!**

"PHEW!"

SNIFF SNIFF

BEING HIT BY A BOLT OF LIGHTNING OR ELECTRICITY ... IS DRAWN WITH **JAGGED LINES**

ZAP

● CHECK OUT YOUR OWN FAVOURITE COMICS, BOOKS AND MAGAZINES FOR OTHER CARTOONISTS' SPECIAL WAYS OF SHOWING THESE THINGS, AND ALSO FOR NEW IDEAS!

COMIC

AND, OF COURSE, YOU CAN **INVENT** YOUR OWN AS WELL!

FROM TIME TO TIME YOU NEED TO SHARPEN UP YOUR DRAWING SKILLS. TO HELP YOU DO THIS I HAVE DEVISED A SERIES OF...

...WHiZZ WORKOUTS!

...READY, STEADY...

DRAW!

THESE WORKOUTS WILL HELP YOU DEVELOP YOUR DRAWING SKILLS AND YOUR IMAGINATION →

FIRST OFF – LET'S MESS AROUND WITH SOME NUMBERS! DON'T WORRY THERE'S NO MATHS INVOLVED, AND NO EXAM AT THE END!

FIRST – PICK A NUMBER FROM 1 TO 9.

NEXT – TURN THAT NUMBER INTO A FACE OR A CARTOON CHARACTER...

6 FOR EXAMPLE

DON'T JUST SIT THERE – TRY IT!!

YOU CAN ALSO DO THIS **WORKOUT** WITH **LETTERS** OF THE ALPHABET...

• WHY NOT TRY THIS WORKOUT WITH SHAPES OR RANDOM SCRIBBLES TOO?!

ANOTHER GREAT WAY TO KEEP YOUR DRAWING ABILITY **IN TRIM** IS TO DRAW **QUICKLY**. IN THIS **WORKOUT** YOU DEVELOP **SPEED**, BECAUSE YOU HAVE TO DRAW THINGS IN JUST **30 SECONDS!**

SO — SIT DOWN SOMEWHERE WITH YOUR SKETCHBOOK, AND DRAW SOME OF THE THINGS YOU SEE AROUND YOU — BUT YOU MUST DRAW EVERY ITEM IN LESS THAN **30 SECONDS!** ... GO!

... 2½ MINUTES LATER ...

COLLECT THESE TOGETHER SO THAT WHEN YOU NEED TO DRAW CARTOONS IN A PARTICULAR SETTING, YOU HAVE ALL THE INSPIRATION YOU NEED!

SOME OTHER IDEAS...

* TAKE **CAPTIONS** FROM YOUR FAVOURITE CARTOONS, AND DRAW COMPLETELY **DIFFERENT** CARTOONS USING THESE 'BORROWED' CAPTIONS.

HERE ARE SOME EXAMPLES YOU COULD TRY...

- ARE YOU SURE IT'S **SAFE?**

- LOOK OUT, HE'S BEHIND YOU!

- YEAH?! YOU AND WHOSE ARMY??

- WE'RE IN TROUBLE NOW - HERE'S HIS MUM!

- TAKE ME TO YOUR LEADER...

- WHAT TIME DO YOU CALL THIS?

- THERE MUST BE A PAGE MISSING?!

- FOR THE **LAST** TIME...

* COLLECT SOME OF YOUR OWN AND TRY IT!!

NOW IT'S TIME TO PUT EVERYTHING
WE'VE LEARNED TO **GOOD USE** . . .

OVER THE NEXT FEW PAGES WE'LL BE
MAKING SOME . . .

- CRAFTY **CARDS.**

- INSPIRED **INVITATIONS.**

- KRAZY **KITES.**

- POWERFUL **PUPPETS.**

- TREMENDOUS **'T' SHIRTS.**

SO GET **READY** FOR SOME
MARVELLOUS MAKES . . .

. . . **COMING RIGHT UP**

ONE OF THE EASIEST - AND BEST - THINGS YOU CAN DO WITH YOUR NEW FOUND CARTOON DRAWING ABILITY, IS TO MAKE YOUR OWN...

GREETINGS CARDS!

A HAND-MADE CARD IS SOMETHING SPECIAL, THAT EVERYONE WILL APPRECIATE!!

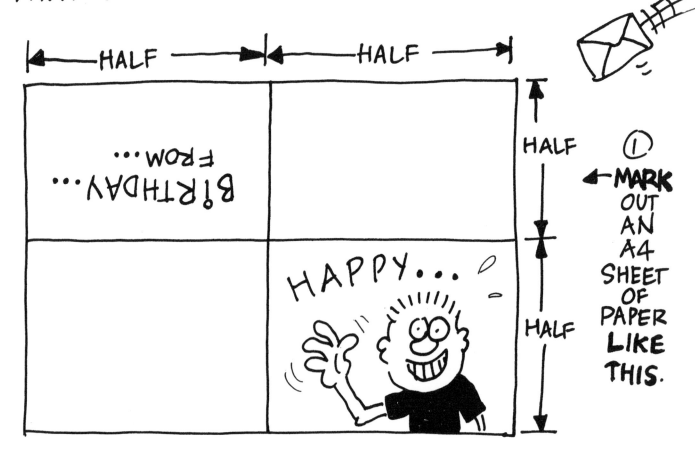

② **DRAW** THE PICTURE AND WRITE THE GREETING AS SHOWN ABOVE.

③ **FOLD** THE CARD ALONG THE LONG EDGE, THEN THE SHORT ONE. NOW - **SEND** IT!

ANOTHER **SIMPLE** TO MAKE **CARD** ALSO USES A SINGLE SHEET OF **A4** PAPER...

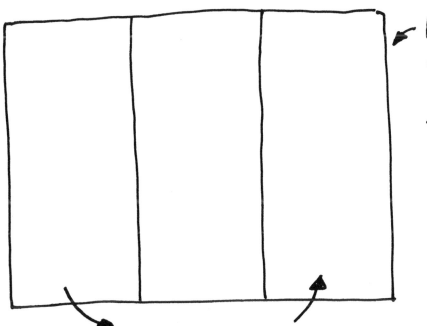

FOLD A SHEET OF A4 PAPER INTO EQUAL THIRDS - TO MAKE A **3** PANEL CARD

FOLD ONE THIRD FORWARD AND THE OTHER THIRD BACK, TO MAKE A **Z** SHAPE.

ROSES ARE RED...

THE FOLDED CARD LOOKS LIKE **THIS**.

1. ROSES ARE RED...

2. VIOLETS ARE BLUE...

3. I HOPE YOU LIKE ME, 'COS I LIKE YOU!

THEY DON'T HAVE TO BE THIS SLOPPY!!

HERE IS A **FULL-SIZE** VERSION! PHOTOCOPY OR TRACE THIS, CUT OUT AND SEND!!

IF YOU WANT TO MAKE A REALLY SPECIAL JOB OF IT, WHY NOT ADD SOME **COLOUR**?!

USE FELT-TIP PENS, PAINTS OR COLOURED PENCILS.

TRY A FEW OF **YOUR** OWN IDEAS.

IF YOU NEED A **LOT** OF CARDS - FOR CHRISTMAS PERHAPS - HAVE YOUR DRAWING PHOTOCOPIED, THEN FOLD AND SEND!

PUSH YOUR CARD CREATING SKILLS TO THE LIMIT WITH THIS...

...MONSTER POP-UP!

COPY THE IMAGE I'VE DRAWN HERE OR DRAW YOUR OWN →

* ADD PLENTY OF SCARS AND STITCHES TO MAKE A TRULY HORRIBLE FACE!

WOLFMAN MUMMY DRACULA AND MORE...

DRAW A MONSTER FACE, FOLD DOWN THE DOTTED LINE AND GLUE THE "BOLTS" ONTO A SHEET OF A4 PAPER, FOLDED DOWN THE MIDDLE.

WHEN YOU CLOSE THE CARD THE FACE FOLDS NEATLY UP INSIDE ~ AND SPRINGS OUT WHEN THE CARD IS OPENED!

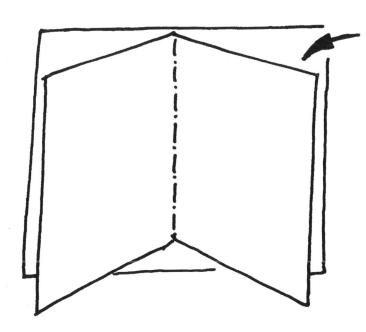

A SHEET OF FAIRLY STIFF A4 PAPER, FOLDED IN THE MIDDLE, MAKES THE BACKING SHEET.

THE FACE FOLDS FORWARD — THE CARD FOLDS BACK. 133

WHY NOT **FRAME** YOUR BEST CARTOONS?!

● YOU CAN BUY INEXPENSIVE FRAMES OR MAKE YOUR **OWN** . . .

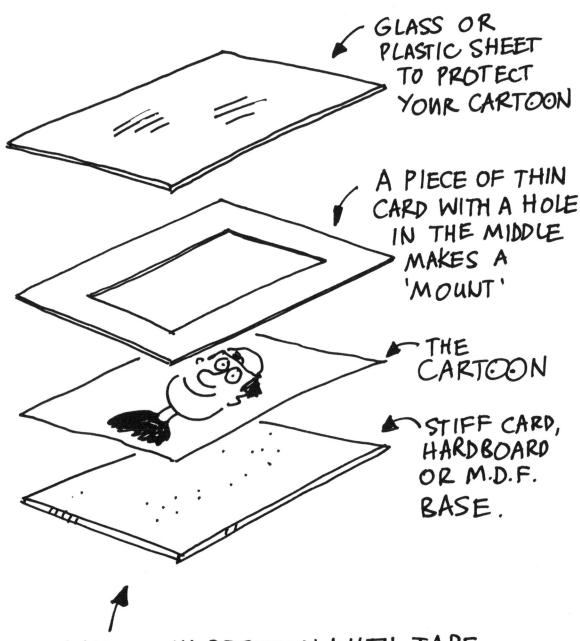

GLASS OR PLASTIC SHEET TO PROTECT YOUR CARTOON

A PIECE OF THIN CARD WITH A HOLE IN THE MIDDLE MAKES A 'MOUNT'

THE CARTOON

STIFF CARD, HARDBOARD OR M.D.F. BASE.

✳ FIX THE LAYERS IN POSITION WITH TAPE OR FRAME CLIPS - FIX A HANGER TO THE BACK - HEY **PRESTO** . . .

THE START OF YOUR VERY **OWN** ART GALLERY!

A GREAT WAY OF SHOWING OFF YOUR CARTOONS IS TO PUT THEM ONTO...

KITES

THERE ARE LOTS OF DIFFERENT KITE SHAPES - THE ONE SHOWN HERE IS A "DIAMOND".

* IF YOU DON'T FANCY MAKING A KITE - BUY A WHITE ONE AND COLOUR IT WITH FABRIC PAINTS!

① CUT 2 STICKS - 75 CM AND 55 CM (29.5" X 21.5") FASTEN INTO A CROSS 19 CM (7.5") FROM THE TOP OF THE LONGER STICK. TIE STRING ALL ROUND THE EDGE OF THE CROSS. ② GLUE A PAPER COVERING ON THE FINISHED DIAMOND SHAPE. ③

FIX A 1 METRE LENGTH OF STRING FROM TOP TO BOTTOM STICKS AND MAKE A LOOP 20 CM (7.8") ABOVE THE JOINT OF THE CROSS — TIE YOUR FLYING LINE TO THIS LOOP AND ENJOY!

* FLY SAFELY - AWAY FROM OVERHEAD OBSTRUCTIONS AND NEVER IN THE RAIN!

MAKE A LONG TAIL FROM PAPER BOWS, TO KEEP THE KITE STABLE. ABOUT 5 METRES WILL DO!

ADD THE DESIGN OF YOUR CHOICE

135

WHY NOT MAKE A SIMPLE **PUPPET!**

DRAW AND CUT OUT A HEAD AND BODY SHAPE. ADD ARMS, HANDS, LEGS AND FEET. FIX STRINGS TO HEAD AND ELBOWS AND YOU'VE GOT IT!

FIX THE PARTS TOGETHER WITH PAPER FASTENERS (BUY THESE FROM A STATIONERY SHOP).

CUT THE SHAPES FROM STIFF CARD AND YOUR PUPPET WILL LAST QUITE A LONG TIME.

MAKE A FEW OF YOUR FAMILY, FRIENDS OR "FAVE" POP STARS OR FOOTBALLERS!

YOU CAN MAKE THEM AS LARGE OR AS SMALL AS YOU LIKE. LIFE SIZE IF YOU CAN FIND ENOUGH CARD AND BIG ENOUGH FASTENERS!

MAKE HOLES HERE FOR JOINING.

136

...HERE'S ANOTHER **NEAT** IDEA...

WHY NOT MAKE A
MOBILE
FROM ALL YOUR CARTOONS?

THE CARTOONS CAN BE ANY SIZE OR SHAPE, AND THE HANGING FRAME CAN BE ANY SIZE!

PASTE YOUR SPARE CARTOONS ON THIN CARD AND HANG FROM THE CEILING.

USE * DOWEL, CANE OR WIRE

* GLUE OR TIE THE STICKS TOGETHER TO MAKE THE HANGING FRAME.

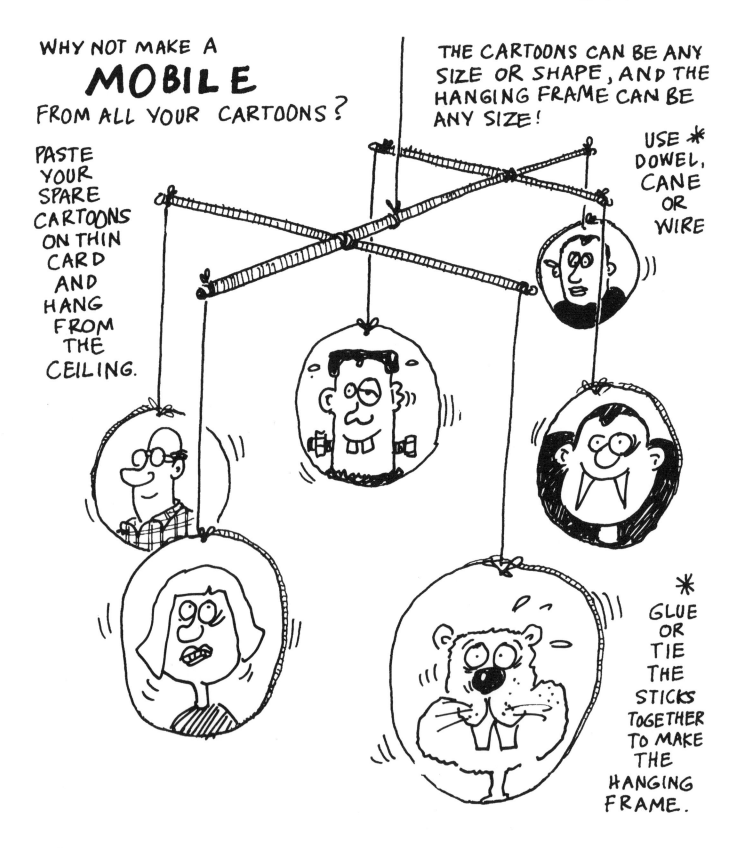

I'M SURE THAT YOU WILL THINK UP EVEN MORE WAYS TO DISPLAY YOUR CARTOONING TALENTS ONCE YOU GET STARTED...

138

NEXT TIME YOU HAVE A PARTY, WHY NOT CREATE YOUR OWN -ORIGINAL- INVITATIONS!?!

COME TO OUR "PARTY"

JUNE 6th AT STEVE'S

6 → LATE!

BRING A FRIEND!

* MAKE SURE YOU INCLUDE ALL THE ESSENTIAL INFORMATION •••

- DATE
- TIME
- LOCATION
- SPECIAL INSTRUCTIONS

GRAND RED-NOSE PARTY!
AT STEVE AND JENNY'S PLACE
SATURDAY MAY 10th 6 -12pm
BRING YOUR RED HOOTER!

YOU CAN CREATE INVITATIONS FOR JUST ABOUT ANYTHING!

FRANK'S FAB FISH ɴᴅ CHIP PARTY!

JUNE 12th
7 – 10pm at
FRANK'S PLAICE!
BRING SALT AND VINEGAR...

● MAKE SURE THAT YOUR FINISHED DESIGN FITS INTO A STANDARD SIZE ENVELOPE – UNLESS YOU ARE GOING TO MAKE THEM AS WELL!

70's DISCO, MAN!
AT CAROLINE'S PAD
Er... JUNE 12th 8 'TIL LATE
BRING A FRIEND AND
BE GROOVY... COOL! PEACE!

ONE GREAT WAY OF SHOWING YOUR FAB DRAWING SKILLS TO AS MANY PEOPLE AS POSSIBLE IS TO PUT YOUR CARTOON ON A...

'T' SHIRT...

● START OUT WITH A PLAIN WHITE 'T' SHIRT ➜

* CUT A PIECE OF STIFF CARD TO FIT INSIDE THE AREA YOU ARE GOING TO 'DECORATE'

CARD...

(THIS STOPS THE FRONT AND BACK OF THE 'T' SHIRT STICKING TOGETHER)

NOW - DRAW YOUR DESIGN ONTO THE SHIRT, AND COLOUR IT WITH FABRIC PENS OR PAINTS ... AND REMEMBER,

FOLLOW THE INSTRUCTIONS THAT COME WITH YOUR COLOURS CAREFULLY!

START WITH SOMETHING SIMPLE ➜

SOME COMPUTER PRINTERS USE A SPECIAL TYPE OF PAPER – WHICH ALLOWS YOU TO IRON A DRAWING ONTO A 'T' SHIRT – **BRILLIANT!**

● AN EASY WAY TO TRANSFER PHOTOCOPIES IS TO USE A TRANSFER FLUID – ASK AT YOUR ART MATERIALS SHOP...

* PICK YOUR METHOD AND LET'S START...

ON THE SUBJECT OF COMPUTERS... THERE ARE NOW A NUMBER OF TERRIFIC CARTOON DRAWING PROGRAMMES FOR A WIDE VARIETY OF COMPUTERS...

SOME OF THEM ENABLE YOU TO PRINT OUT YOUR DRAWINGS, OTHERS PRINT 'T' SHIRTS, SOME WILL EVEN MAKE SHORT ANIMATIONS!!

YOU CAN CONNECT SOME COMPUTERS TO A CAMCORDER TO MAKE ANIMATIONS.

COMPUTERS ARE USED IN MANY CARTOON STUDIOS, AND NEW THINGS ARE BEING ADDED ALL THE TIME!

YOU CAN USE YOUR CARTOONING ABILITY
TO CREATE AND PLAY SOME GREAT

"GAMES"...

● HERE'S AN **EASY** GAME YOU CAN **MAKE**...

① CUT SOME A4 SHEETS INTO THIRDS —
LIKE THIS

② DRAW A CARTOON
FIGURE ON EACH
PIECE...

③ NOW—CUT EACH
FIGURE INTO
4 SECTIONS..
  ● HEAD
  ● BODY
  ● LEGS
  ● FEET

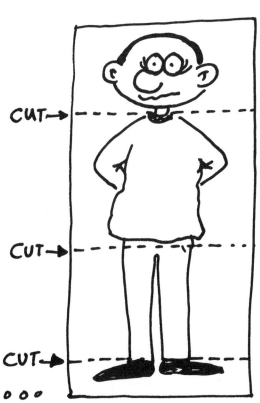

CUT→
CUT→
CUT→

144

✳
NOW TO PLAY THE GAME...

PUT ALL THE PIECES **FACE-DOWN** ON A TABLE - AND WRITE THESE NUMBERS ON THE **BACK**...

2 - ON THE HEADS

3 - ON THE BODIES

4 - ON THE LEGS

5 - ON THE FEET

NOW - FIND A **DICE** AND ROLL IT IN **TURNS**...

IF YOU ROLL A 1 OR A 6 YOU MISS A TURN, IF YOU ROLL A 2, 3, 4 OR 5 YOU PICK UP A PIECE FROM THE TABLE.

WHEN ALL THE PIECES HAVE BEEN **USED-UP**, THE PERSON WHO ASSEMBLED THE MOST COMPLETE FIGURES IS THE **WINNER**...

* OF COURSE IT DOESN'T MATTER IF ALL THE PARTS **MATCH** OR NOT - IT'S ALL PART OF THE **FUN!**

CARTOON CONSEQUENCES...

IS ANOTHER GREAT GAME - AND ALL YOU NEED TO **PLAY** IT IS A PENCIL AND PAPER...

CUT

CUT A SHEET OF A4 PAPER DOWN THE LONG EDGE. (THIS WILL GIVE YOU 2 STRIPS - SO YOU CAN PLAY **TWICE!**)

THEN - THE FIRST PLAYER DRAWS A HEAD AT THE TOP OF THE STRIP, THEN FOLDS THE PAPER OVER SO THE DRAWING IS HIDDEN...

FOLD OVER TO HIDE CARTOON HEAD

THE NEXT PLAYER DRAWS THE BODY, FOLDS IT OVER, AND HANDS IT TO THE NEXT PERSON

146

THE NEXT PERSON DRAWS THE LEGS, AND THE
LAST PERSON DRAWS THE FEET - EACH TIME
FOLDING THE PAPER TO HIDE THEIR PART!

WHEN ALL
THE DRAWING
IS DONE –

OPEN OUT THE
PAPER AND
SHARE YOUR
JOINT
MASTERPIECE
WITH THE
WORLD!

* THE MORE
YOU HAVE IN
THIS GAME THE
FUNNIER IT
GETS!!

CARTOON CONSEQUENCES IS A GREAT **PARTY** GAME TOO!

FOLD A SHEET OF A4 PAPER INTO THREE EQUAL STRIPS, AND WE'LL **MAKE** A FREAKY

FACE FOLDER...

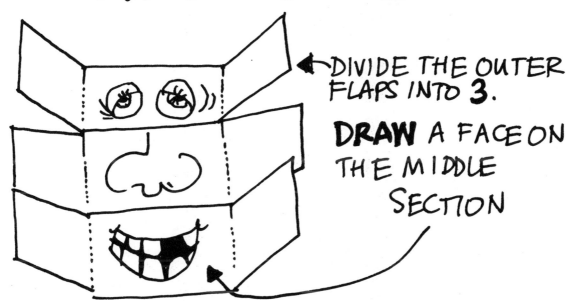

← DIVIDE THE OUTER FLAPS INTO **3**.

DRAW A FACE ON THE MIDDLE SECTION

THEN...
GET A COUPLE OF **FRIENDS** TO DRAW FACES ON THE OTHER TWO FLAPS — BUT KEEP YOUR OWN DRAWING COVERED.

THEN **CUT** THE SIDE FLAPS INTO THREE . LIKE THE EXAMPLE ABOVE. AND **FOLD!**

● YOU CAN DRAW FACES ONLY — OR USE LARGER SHEETS OF PAPER AND DO WHOLE **BODIES!!** ☺

MORE, MORE →

TECHNICAL STUFF...?

PUZZLED BY PENS?
BOTHERED BY BRUSHES?
PERPLEXED BY PAPER SIZES?
* WORRY NO MORE! OVER THE NEXT FEW
PAGES I WILL EXPLAIN ALL THE ESSENTIAL
INFORMATION YOU NEED TO KNOW TO
CONVERSE IN FLUENT "CARTOONSPEAK"

PAPER, PENS AND PENCILS...

WHAT SIZE SHOULD I USE??

PAPER...

USE WHATEVER PAPER SIZE SUITS YOUR OWN STYLE. CUT DOWN LARGE SHEETS IF YOU PREFER WORKING SMALL!

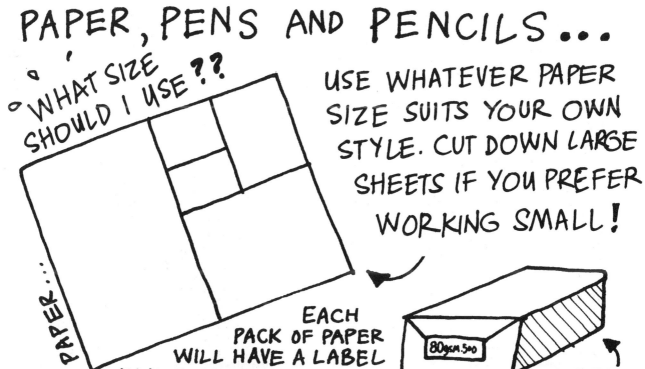

EACH PACK OF PAPER WILL HAVE A LABEL WHICH TELLS YOU THE SIZE AND WEIGHT.

80gsm.500

A REAM OF PAPER IS 500 SHEETS.

g.s.m IS THE WEIGHT MEASURE OF PAPER. 80 TO 120 g.s.m. WILL BE IDEAL FOR ALL THE PROJECTS IN THIS BOOK.

PENS...

'TECHNICAL' PENS ARE SOLD IN VARIOUS SIZES:

0.1 0.2 0.3 0.4
0.5 0.6 0.7 0.8
0.9 1.0 1.2 ETC.

TO WRITE AND ILLUSTRATE THIS BOOK I USED—

0.6 0.8 AND 1.0 SIZES.

TECHNICAL PENS TAKE INK CARTRIDGES OR HAVE REFILLABLE INK FACILITIES.

PENS NEED TO BE KEPT CLEAN!

PENCILS...

THE CHART BELOW SHOWS HOW PENCILS ARE GRADED IN HARD AND SOFT TYPES. I USE A GRADE "B".

← HARDER
2H
3H   H   HB   B   2B   4B
                        3B

SOFTER →
*

USE INDIAN INK IN "DIP" PENS, AND WASH THE NIB AFTERWARDS — DON'T USE THIS INK IN FOUNTAIN PENS AS IT WILL CLOG THEM UP!

TYPING CORRECTION FLUID WILL COVER UP YOUR MISTAKES

AND A SOFT PLASTIC ERASER WILL REMOVE PENCIL LINES WITHOUT SCRATCHING THE PAPER

BLACK INK

TIP ZAP

MOST FOUNTAIN PENS CAN ALSO BE CONVERTED TO TAKE INK CARTRIDGES.

A PENCIL SHARPENER WILL KEEP YOUR PENCILS READY FOR ACTION!

ALWAYS WORK IN GOOD LIGHT — FROM A READING LAMP OR A WINDOW

YOU DON'T **NEED A** DRAWING BOARD — ANY FIRM SURFACE WILL BE FINE!

PRACTICE PAGE...

HERE ARE SOME FACES FOR YOU TO FINISH...

TRACE OR COPY THESE PART-FINISHED FACES, AND SEE WHAT YOU CAN DO WITH THEM !?

PRACTICE PAGE •••

HERE ARE SOME HANDS AND FEET FOR YOU TO FINISH •••

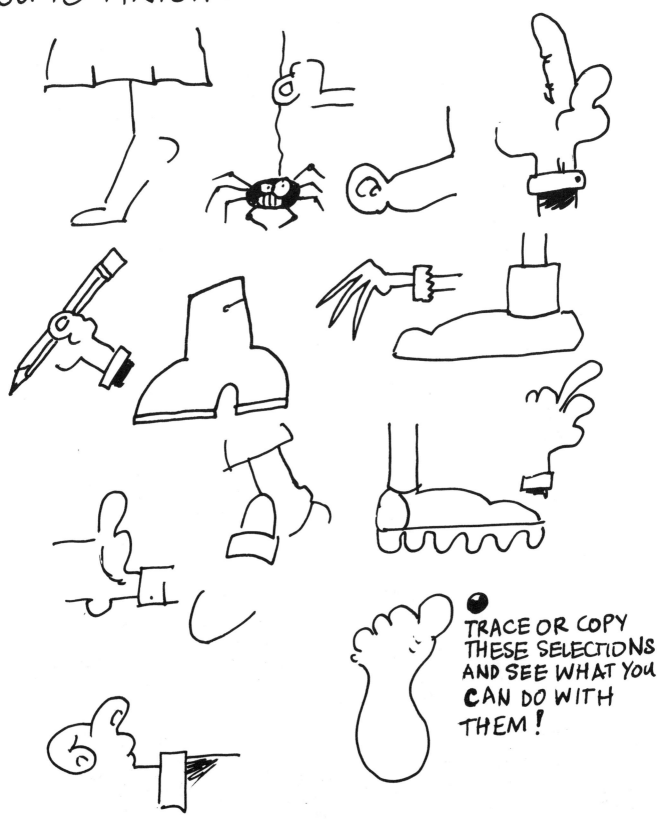

TRACE OR COPY THESE SELECTIONS AND SEE WHAT YOU CAN DO WITH THEM!

PRACTICE PAGE ...

TRACE OR COPY THESE
'BODY BITS' AND SEE
HOW BRILLIANTLY
YOU CAN FINISH
THEM ...

PRACTICE PAGE ...

HERE ARE SOME 'ORRIBLE ODDS AND ENDS FOR YOU TO ASSEMBLE INTO SOMETHING SCARY! EEK!!

● TRACE OR COPY THESE MONSTER PARTS AND SEE WHAT YOU CAN CREATE FROM THEM...

...HUR, HUR, HUR...

WHAT **SIZE** SHOULD I **DRAW?**

● IF YOU ARE DRAWING CARTOONS FOR YOUR OWN ENJOYMENT IT DOESN'T MATTER WHAT SIZE YOU DRAW. I USE A4 SIZED PAPER ALL THE TIME, AND AN AVERAGE CARTOON WILL USE ABOUT HALF THE PAGE →

CARTOONS USED IN NEWSPAPERS, BOOKS AND MAGAZINES ARE USUALLY DRAWN 1½ OR 2 TIMES LARGER - THEN REDUCED BY THE PRINTER TO THE FINISHED SIZE.

COMIC PAGES NEED TO BE LARGER, TO ENABLE YOU TO INCLUDE LOTS OF DETAIL - SO USE A3 SIZE PAPER IF POSSIBLE.

● MOST CARDS CAN BE MADE WITH A4 PAPER, AND SHOULD FIT AN A5 SIZE ENVELOPE WHEN FOLDED.

● EXPERIMENT WITH DIFFERENT SIZES, AND USE WHATEVER FEELS 'RIGHT' FOR YOU!

AFTER ALL - THEY'RE YOUR CARTOONS!

WHAT **NEXT** ?!?

NOW THAT YOU HAVE LEARNED THE ESSENTIAL SKILLS OF CARTOONING, I HOPE THAT YOU WILL WANT TO PRACTISE AT EVERY OPPORTUNITY.

START BY MAKING A THANK-YOU CARD FOR THE PERSON WHO BOUGHT YOU THIS BOOK—WHAT A WISE PURCHASE!

IF YOU ARE A STUDENT—USE YOUR SKILLS TO PRESENT EVEN BETTER WORK BY ADDING A FEW DRAWINGS HERE AND THERE.

IF YOU WANT TO TAKE YOUR CARTOON DRAWING EVEN FURTHER, CONSIDER DOING A FULL CARTOONING COURSE....

WRITE TO ME HERE

THE CARTOON SCHOOL
PROSPECT COACH HOUSE
HIGH LANE
HIGH BIRSTWITH
HARROGATE
HG3 2JL
ENGLAND

HOW TO USE YOUR "SUPER" STENCILS

THE STENCILS PROVIDED WITH THIS BOOK ARE A **GREAT** WAY TO START CARTOONING.

SIMPLY PLACE THE STENCILS ON A SHEET OF DRAWING PAPER, AND DRAW CAREFULLY AROUND THE INSIDE EDGE –

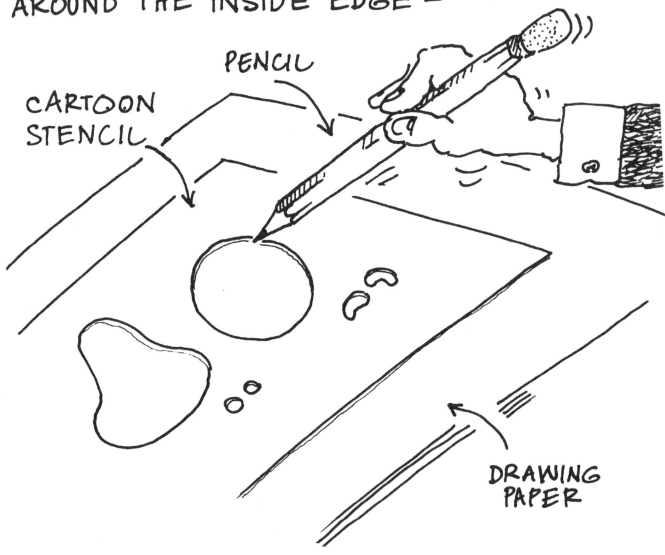

PENCIL

CARTOON STENCIL

DRAWING PAPER

ALWAYS KEEP YOUR STENCILS IN A SAFE PLACE AND HANDLE THEM CAREFULLY.

OVER THE NEXT FEW PAGES WE WILL LEARN HOW TO USE THESE STENCILS TO CREATE A COLLECTION OF CRAZY CARTOON CHARACTERS **!**

HERE WE GO, HERE WE GO ...

REMEMBER TO DRAW THE WHOLE CARTOON IN
PENCIL TO BEGIN WITH, AND THEN DRAW
IN INK WHEN YOU HAVE ADDED ALL THE PARTS
YOU WANT TO INCLUDE IN YOUR CARTOON...

YOU WILL FIND SHAPES FOR FACES, EYES,
HAIR, HANDS, FEET, BODIES AND ACCESSORIES ON
THE STENCILS —

WHEN THE INK IS DRY CAREFULLY ERASE
THE PENCIL LINES. NOW YOU CAN ADD
OTHER CARTOON CHARACTERS, COLOUR YOUR
CARTOON, MAKE IT INTO A COMIC PAGE OR
USE IT TO CREATE A NUMBER OF FUN
THINGS FOR YOURSELF, FAMILY OR FRIENDS.

LET'S BEGIN WITH A SIMPLE HAPPY FACE...

DRAW THE HEAD SHAPE
TO BEGIN WITH —
(REMEMBER TO DRAW IN
PENCIL AT FIRST).

NEXT ADD SOME ROUND
EYE SHAPES — AND DRAW
A LITTLE DOT IN THE
MIDDLE OF EACH EYE.

NOW WE ADD THE NOSE.

AND THEN THE
HAPPY MOUTH.

✳
OUR FIRST CARTOON!

OUR SIMPLE HAPPY FACE CAN BE MALE OR FEMALE SIMPLY BY ADDING DIFFERENT HAIRSTYLES.

YOU CAN FILL THE HAIR SHAPE WITH BLACK INK, OR JUST SKETCH IN A FEW LINES FOR LIGHTER HAIR COLOUR.

WHERE YOU WANT EARS SIMPLY WRITE THE NUMBER 3 ON THE RIGHT SIDE OF THE HEAD, AND A REVERSED NUMBER Ɛ ON THE LEFT.

EXPERIMENT WITH EXTRA FEATURES LIKE EYELASHES, LIPSTICK AND EARRINGS ON FEMALE FACES.

BY ADDING A LINE ALONG THE MIDDLE OF THE MOUTH SHAPE WE CAN CREATE TEETH!

A SAD FACE CAN USE THE SMILING MOUTH — UPSIDE DOWN...

HERE I HAVE ALSO USED THE CURVED EYES →

THESE EYES LOOK READY TO CRY!!

YOU CAN USE THE ROUND EYES ON A SAD FACE IF YOU DRAW A LINE ACROSS THE MIDDLE, LIKE THIS →

IN THIS SAD FACE I HAVE USED THE CURVED MOUTH →

I HAVE JUST USED A SINGLE LINE FOR THIS → SAD MOUTH

NOW — IT'S YOUR TURN!

TRY A FEW SAD FACES OF YOUR OWN — THEN WE WILL DRAW SOME ANGRY ONES!!

AN ANGRY FACE USES THE TRIANGLE SHAPED EYES AND THE WAVY MOUTH.

YOU CAN ALSO ADD SOME LINES ON THE FOREHEAD OF AN ANGRY FACE.

IN THIS ANGRY FACE I HAVE ALSO ADDED SOME LINES UNDER THE EYES TO GIVE THE IMPRESSION OF "FLUSHED" CHEEKS!

IF WE REPLACE THE WAVY MOUTH WITH THE SMILING MOUTH WE GET A SLY, CRAFTY FACE - PLOTTING REVENGE !!

DON'T BE AFRAID TO TRY CRAZY COMBINATIONS OF FACIAL FEATURES - JUST FOR **FUN** !

SOME OTHER FACES YOU MIGHT LIKE TO
HAVE A TRY AT...

A TIRED OR
BORED FACE.

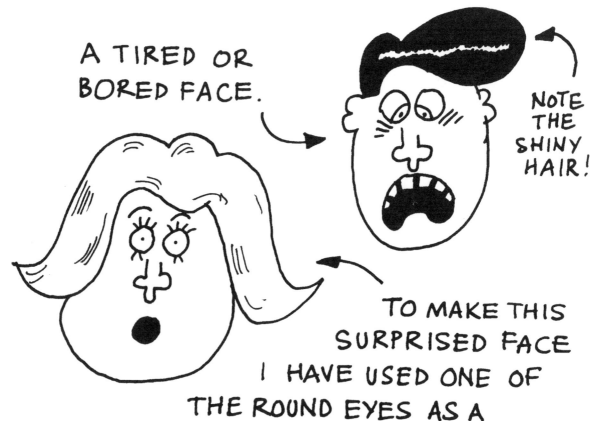

NOTE
THE
SHINY
HAIR!

TO MAKE THIS
SURPRISED FACE
I HAVE USED ONE OF
THE ROUND EYES AS A
MOUTH — AND DRAWN TWO SMALL CURVES
ABOVE THE EYES FOR RAISED EYEBROWS!

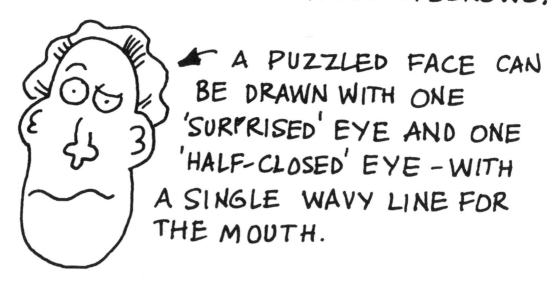

A PUZZLED FACE CAN
BE DRAWN WITH ONE
'SURPRISED' EYE AND ONE
'HALF-CLOSED' EYE — WITH
A SINGLE WAVY LINE FOR
THE MOUTH.

THERE IS ALMOST NO END TO THE NUMBER
OF FACES YOU CAN CREATE —

TIME FOR A LITTLE **BODY-BUILDING**!

LET'S BEGIN WITH A COUPLE OF SIMPLE FIGURE SHAPES...

HERE I HAVE USED THE BODY AND LEGS, SHOES AND ARMS TO MAKE SOMEONE JUST STANDING AROUND — MAYBE DRINKING A CAN OF POP, PLAYING DARTS OR SPEAKING TO SOMEONE...

BY POINTING BOTH SHOES IN THE SAME DIRECTION YOU GIVE THE IMPRESSION OF ➔ SOMEONE WALKING.

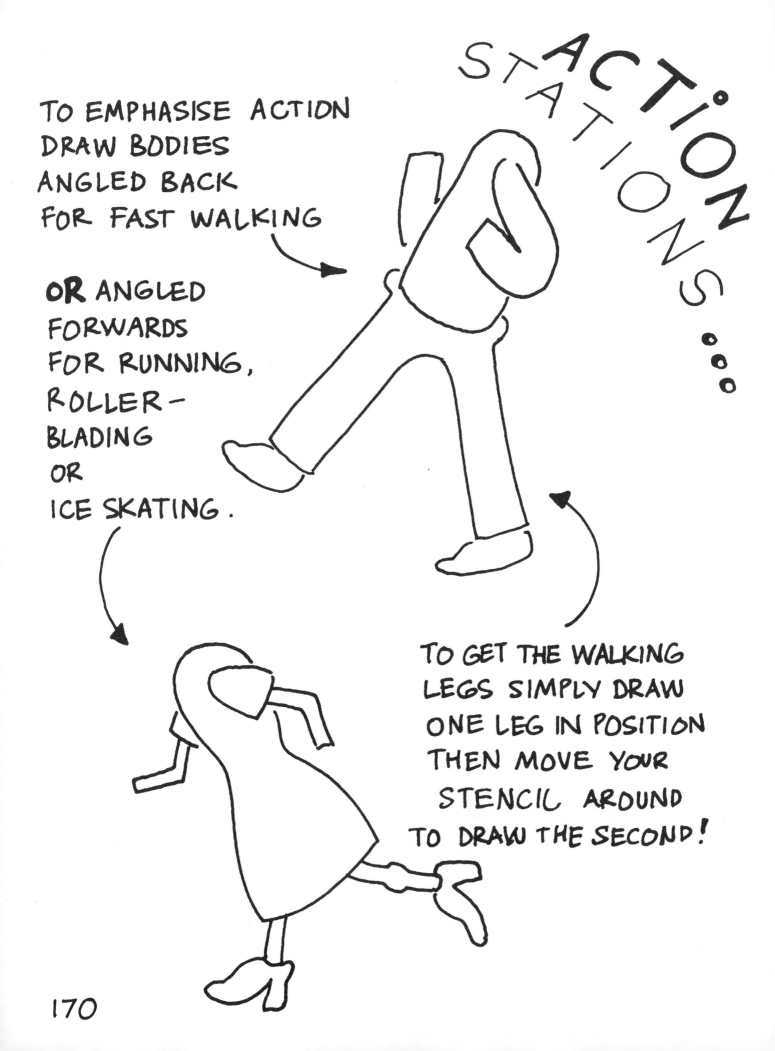

TO EMPHASISE ACTION DRAW BODIES ANGLED BACK FOR FAST WALKING

OR ANGLED FORWARDS FOR RUNNING, ROLLER-BLADING OR ICE SKATING.

ACTION STATIONS...

TO GET THE WALKING LEGS SIMPLY DRAW ONE LEG IN POSITION THEN MOVE YOUR STENCIL AROUND TO DRAW THE SECOND!

TO HELP YOU DRAW EVEN MORE FIGURES
YOU CAN USE A SIMPLE STICK FIGURE -

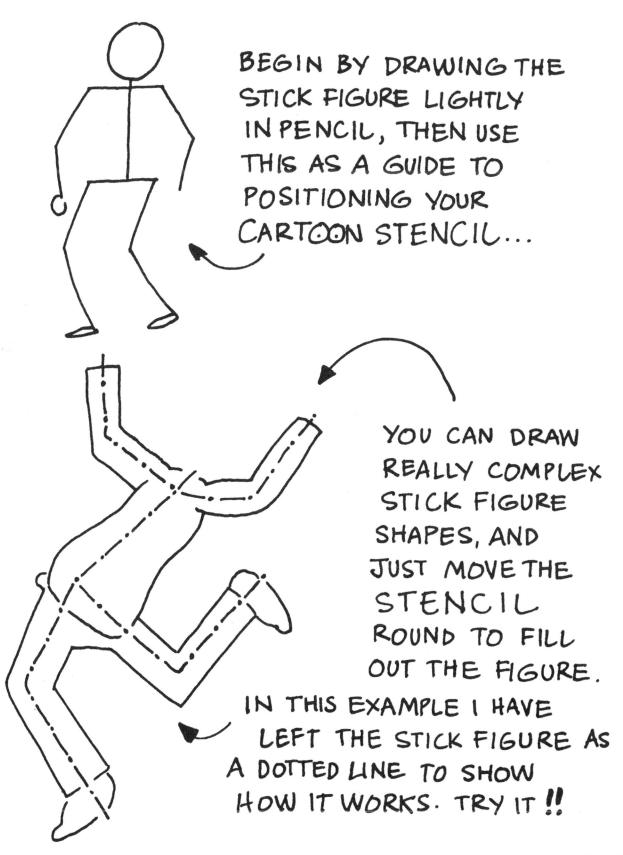

BEGIN BY DRAWING THE
STICK FIGURE LIGHTLY
IN PENCIL, THEN USE
THIS AS A GUIDE TO
POSITIONING YOUR
CARTOON STENCIL...

YOU CAN DRAW
REALLY COMPLEX
STICK FIGURE
SHAPES, AND
JUST MOVE THE
STENCIL
ROUND TO FILL
OUT THE FIGURE.
IN THIS EXAMPLE I HAVE
LEFT THE STICK FIGURE AS
A DOTTED LINE TO SHOW
HOW IT WORKS. TRY IT **!!**

NOW WE CAN PUT THE HEADS AND BODIES TOGETHER ⟶

I USED A STICK FIGURE TO HELP ME CONSTRUCT THIS CARTOON.

✳REMEMBER THAT YOU CAN MAKE ANY PART OF YOUR CARTOON LARGER OR SMALLER DEPENDING ON THE EFFECT YOU REQUIRE.

PRACTISE DRAWING THESE HEAD AND BODY CARTOONS, AND IN THE NEXT SECTION WE WILL DRAW HANDS AND FEET, AND GIVE OUR CARTOON PEOPLE SOME THINGS TO DO!

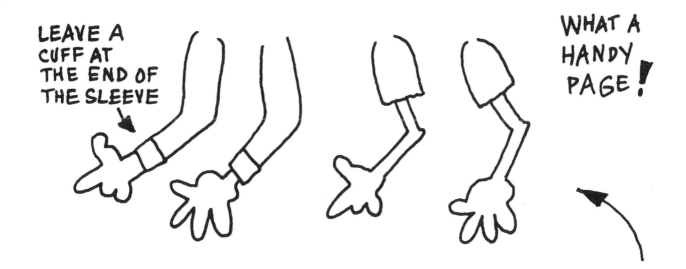

LEAVE A CUFF AT THE END OF THE SLEEVE

WHAT A HANDY PAGE!

THERE ARE SOME SIMPLE HAND SHAPES ON YOUR CARTOON STENCILS THAT WILL GET YOU STARTED, AS IN THE EXAMPLES ABOVE.

TO DRAW A HAND HOLDING SOMETHING FIRST DRAW THE OBJECT THEN DRAW THE HAND - BUT DRAW THE FINGERS POINTING THE OTHER WAY AROUND AND IT WILL LOOK LIKE THE HAND IS GRIPPING THE OBJECT.

YOU CAN — OF COURSE — DRAW YOUR OWN HANDS · · · ·

THERE ARE A COUPLE OF SIMPLE SHOE SHAPES
ON YOUR CARTOON STENCILS WHICH YOU
WILL BE ABLE TO USE FOR A LOT OF YOUR
CARTOONS—

AND YOU CAN ADAPT THESE SIMPLE SHAPES TO
GIVE YOU AN EVEN WIDER RANGE OF
FOOTWEAR • • •

← ADD A THICK SOLE, SOME FANCY
STRIPES AND SPORT SOCKS TO
MAKE TRAINERS.

THICK LACES AND A CHUNKY →
SOLE GIVES YOU HIKING BOOTS

A THIN SOLE AND A TARTAN
PATTERN MAKES SLIPPERS!

ATTACH A BLADE FOR ICE SKATES

* I'M CERTAIN YOU WILL THINK
UP LOTS MORE IDEAS!!

ON YOUR CARTOON STENCIL SHEETS YOU WILL FIND A VARIETY OF 'ACCESSORIES' – THINGS YOU CAN GIVE YOUR CARTOON PEOPLE TO PLAY WITH...

...LIKE THIS SAXOPHONE

CARTOONS ARE ALWAYS MORE INTERESTING IF THE CHARACTERS IN THEM ARE DOING SOMETHING!

* REMEMBER TO CHANGE THE POSE OF YOUR CHARACTER TO SUIT WHAT HE OR SHE IS DOING

IN THE CARTOON ABOVE I HAVE ANGLED THE SAXOPHONE PLAYER'S BODY BACK A LITTLE • • • LET'S TRY A FEW MORE • • • 175

HERE WE HAVE SOMEONE HEADING OFF TO WORK, COMPLETE WITH AN UMBRELLA AND BRIEFCASE. I HAVE FILLED IN THE SHOES, HAIR AND UMBRELLA WITH BLACK INK.

NEXT IS SOMEONE HAVING FUN ?!* I HAVE USED SMALL CIRCLES FOR THE WHEELS OF THE SKATEBOARD. SHE LOOKS A BIT WORRIED — BUT YOU CAN HAVE YOUR CHARACTERS HOWEVER YOU WANT THEM.

NOW... IT'S **YOUR** TURN!

176